MW01634719

A Fair and Timely Warning

The ideas that you find in this work are not necessarily new, but the conclusions drawn are up-to-date, so it should be of great interest to those that are concerned about solving their earthly problems. It may however alienate you from the spiritually-inclined and cause you to walk and think alone in their god-fearing and grovelling midst. It is some of their age-old beliefs and survival values that I discount, and which we must change if our species is to avoid its competitive fate.

When we are young we are taught some history and geography, but mostly reading, writing and arithmetic. Eventually we choose a vocation, which enables us to earn our livelihood and become productive members of society. We learn the wisdom and skills of our age, and as our societies invent new technology; nations compete for survival with more effective and powerful weaponry.

Our wars have been with us since ancient times, and have grown more destructive, expensive, and with much bloodshed and suffering. We must prevent wars from continuing by overcoming the natural forces that drive us to compete. Realizing that our civilization has always progressed at its own speed, I can only describe the direction that we should steer it in. If this causes you to oppose and be injured by the unwieldy thing, the author disclaims any liability whatsoever.

The Author of this Educational Treatise
(and contender for the Nobel Peace Prize)

Preface

The author was the second son of a large family and grew up on a mixed farm in an agricultural community. His first experience of a governing organization in which he played a part was his school's Student Union, which sold tickets to raffles and held a dance in the community hall to raise funds for a bag of goodies and a gift from Santa at the Christmas concert. The bags of goodies consisted of an apple, mandarin oranges, nuts and candy, and each bag contained approximately the same amount. The gifts were selected by two elected senior students and each was of approximately the same value. There was no cause for complaint and everyone enjoyed the festivities.

This sense of fairness prevailed amongst our family and friends, and it was considered an insult to be singled out and treated as inferior to others. A few years after I had quit school I attended a political meeting in this same community hall and found that we had to petition our government for the public services we hoped to receive. These requests were rarely met and it became obvious that those with the most political pull were favored at the expense of the less influential. This was my introduction to our governmental system, and I was disappointed to find that patronage and discriminatory practices were not forbidden.

We lived in Alberta and the voting power was in the east, so with freight subsidies for feed grain and feeder cattle the easterners were able make more money feeding cattle than we were. In effect our jobs were transported east along with our cattle and grain, for with no freight rate assistance for fat cattle we were denied a level playing field. Our local politicians were also profiting by their devious activities--building market roads that always meandered past their own farms and that were not properly positioned to best serve the other residents in the area.

Later I took up the mechanical trade and worked in repair shops in many towns and cities. I found that urban politicians were equally self-serving. After a short stint in a government repair shop, I returned to the family farm and worked in partnership until I was able to buy land nearby. I had gained a fair knowledge of the natural forces that motivated, and the methods by which our species commit and justify their overbearing acts. I was also very critical of the actions of our discriminating and majority-appeasing rulers, but at the time did not have any workable alternatives to offer. My theories have evolved along with my literary ability, and it has taken a lifetime to determine how best to overcome our economic shortages. We cannot solve this problem in one area without solving it in others, and since neither humans nor grasshoppers respect boundaries our remedies must be of a global nature.

The Theory
of
Reality

Samuel Tolsdorf

For permission write to
Leumas Publications
#407 – 334 Carrall Street
Vancouver, B.C., Canada V5B 2J3

Canadian Cataloguing in Publication Data
Tolsdorf, Samuel, 1926–
   The theory of reality
   1. War and civilization. I. Title.
CB481.T64 1998   303.6'6   C98-911183-0

Printed and bound in Canada.

Contents

A Fair and Timely Warning — i

Preface — iii

Dedication — ix

Acknowledgements — x

Introduction — xi

1. The Inquisitive have investigated — 1

2. Salvation is our Challenge — 7

3. The Growth of Knowledge and Technology — 31

4. As I see it — 35

5. Tend to your Marbles — 71

6. The Demon within us — 81

7. Some Rhyme and Reason — 85

8. The Modern Day Robbing Hoods must depart — 91

9. A Review of sorts — 113

10. A Quest for National and Political Unity — 125

11. Goodbye and Good Luck — 129

12. An Afterthought or two — 131

Dedication

(Dedicated to the ill-fated societies of our planet)

Let them use their accumulated knowledge to avoid the conflicts that both nature and human nature subjects them to.

Acknowledgements

I would like to thank all of the broadminded people of today and yesterday. Their views and their writings gave me the grains of wisdom, and the pieces of a picture that I attempt to portray in this work. Also, to the many that helped me in correcting my diction, my misspellings, and my punctuation. Some were amateures, but others were proclaimed professionals. Some charged me for their services, and others did not. Some were able to give me constructive criticism, but most were not. To all of you, even to those that did not give me hope; thank you, for giving me the practice to better explain what is obvious and what is not.

Introduction

We are the new generation and find that we are the dominant species. It is all ours: the resources of the planet, the natural forces that control it, and the hope to improve our prospects while we are here. Our competitive activities are motivated by nature and we can only overcome our civilization's blood-thirstiness by avoiding the need to compete.

The only thing that is mysterious about the powers of nature is that many of them are not visible and clearly understood. This caused the ancients to attribute these powers to that of equally invisible heavenly beings. In those early eras they could not adequately explain the phenomena of which they were a part, and passed on their life skills and legendary beliefs from generation to generation.

Since then we have had thousands of years to study and exploit the forces that seemingly control our destiny. We now realize that our species, as well as all other species on earth are fated to the struggles and strife of the competitive existence that natural circumstances impose upon them. We are the only species that is able to escape from the grip of the ever present powers of nature, or from the hands of the vengeful gods. We need to overcome the competitive existance that we have inherited.

Our misunderstanding of the nature of our problems has prevented us from acting in a positive manner to avoid them. That should and must come to an end, and these discoveries; like parts of a torn map, will test our resolve to find a safe route toward our goal. Some of the pieces of the map are missing, but we can now determine in which direction we wish to go.

1

The Inquisitive Have Investigated

(And as a result, we can now reach conclusions)

Many eons ago a large cloud of dust and gases in one of our galaxy's spiral arms condensed to form our sun and the planets that circle it. After the earth cooled, life established itself and evolved; which is evidenced by the petrified skeletons of past species, as well as by our present life forms. Only within the last few centuries has our collective knowledge advanced sufficiently to explain the forces that were responsible for the formation of our solar system and the evolution of species upon this planet. Scientists of late have catalogued the elements according to their atomic compositions and have discovered that the atoms themselves are composed of many smaller particles. But this is not a story about astronomy, biology, or physics, but of conclusions that can be drawn from the lot of them. In capitalizing upon the discoveries of others, the author makes his own discoveries that are of equal or greater concern.

The human species, evolving as it did to become the most intelligent, has gained the ability to overpower and exterminate all other species. However, competing as we do amongst ourselves, and with the use of our cunning and modern weaponry, we have become the most aggressive and fearsome creatures to have ever roamed upon the face of the earth. We have taken or destroyed the life-supporting resources of other species and caused them to die out. We have domesticated the horse, the cow, and the chicken to exploit for our convenience. We have been able to counteract and cure illnesses, improve nutrition, and increase our lifespan. In our quest to exploit all that is before us we only meet a worthy opponent when we fight amongst ourselves, or when our societies or nations war against each other. Then the strongest or most technically advanced, in gaining control of the assets of the defeated, impose their own rules to advantage themselves.

We have seen this when a socialist state confiscates all private property for its own needs. In earlier times, the Europeans discovered Africa, Australia, and the Americas, and their nation claimed the territories they found. In order to exploit them to greater advantage they encouraged their citizens to migrate to the newly established colonies. They allotted free land to settlers that were willing to put it into agricultural production. In this way the nation could tax their properties to get a share of the producers earnings. The invading hordes decimated the wild game that the hunting and gathering tribes relied upon for subsistence, and so reduced their numbers. With the confiscation of territory and the depletion of nature's provisions on the remainder, the surviving native populations are faced with the necessity to accept the productive ways of the industrious societies that overwhelmed them.

It is those that utilize modern methods that are the most productive and efficient. They are able to outpopulate and overpower the less efficient. They are the force that determines the course of civilization. By inventing and using better tools and techniques our civilization advances. It is propelled by the combined efforts of people to achieve a secure and comfortable economic position in life. Some are forced to contribute more sweat than others in order to compete successfully for survival. As yet, our modern societies have not been able to recognize and overcome the earthly influences that drive them to instinctively compete against each other. As a result, our civilization remains unguided by human intellect; and subjects all of us to the perils of the arms race, and a destiny that is not of our choosing.

We are driven by competition to become more efficient and to gain greater prosperity in order to remain dominant. This competition between humans, or amongst individual members of any species, is nature's way of selecting who shall flourish and who shall perish. The need to compete for survival has caused us to evolve both physically and mentally, and we could thank the forces of nature for our presence or blame them for the predicaments they have brought upon us.

We are slowly but surely depleting our earth's natural resources; contaminating our air, water, and soils, and consequently destroying our life-support systems. However; we could do it much faster by allowing our major competitions to continue, and using the atomic weapons that we have manufactured for the job. We have advanced our knowledge of the environment and have discovered that gravity is the natural force that controls the orbit of our temperate planet and keeps us from falling off. The heat of the sun causes the circulation of the air, the evaporation of moisture, and consequently is responsible for our weather patterns. The tilt of our planet as well as a slight orbital variation causes our seasonal temperature changes. The heat that is generated within the earth keeps its interior molten, and the movement of the earth's plates causes our continents to drift. Other forces are electro-magnetic and the strong and the weak nuclear forces which keep our atoms and their numerous particles together. Knowing all this, leads to the realization that life is not controlled by higher intelligences (as the ancients believed) but by forces that are now explainable and predictable; and which we in this enlightened age, can and should take into consideration in directing our daily lives and in guiding the course of civilization.

Life on earth is believed to have begun through a combination of nonorganic atoms in our ancient seas, creating a single-celled organism that was capable of reproducing itself. From this early beginning, mutation and evolution brought forth living organisms in ever-increasing complexity, and the less fit were crowded out as the food that sustained them was taken by those that were more adaptable and vigorous. These same evolutionary pressures have brought humanity its physical and mental attributes, giving our species the ability to take command of the earth's resources and defy all others. This has made us the beneficiaries of all that is before us, but regrettably we have not as yet put our intelligence to use in avoiding the toll that natural circumstances and our own instinctive competitivenesses are inflicting upon us.

All life forms on earth are capable of reproducing more of their own kind, and so continue from generation to generation. All species propagate in abundance, and the meagre provisions of nature and the limitations of our planetary area cannot provide sufficient sustenance for all. Therefore, through competition, the foolish, the infirm, and the poorly- designed perish;

allowing species through natural selection and mutation to evolve both physically and mentally.

Humans have been free to reproduce and multiply within the sanctions of their society, for an abundant population has been essential to a nation's survival. In many instances they have also been legally prevented from using certain devices, drugs, or procedures in preventing pregnancies and births; for a society has had to maintain its might in order to retard their rivals. Our competitions for the resources of the earth and its ecological destruction by the exploitation of excessive populations should be prevented. Therefore, we must avoid the fate that natural conditions subjects us to by uniting the nations and regulate our numbers; giving us plentiful resources to exploit and prosper peacefully upon.

In the following chapters, I disclose the methods by which we can halt our competitions for the earth's real estate and the earnings of others' labors. Let us hope that our might becomes tempered with wisdom, and that our wisdom leads us to our salvation.

Theodore Kaczinski's Nemesis
(And a few more harebrained responses
to an impending event)

2

Salvation Is Our Challenge

(For those that have the time and the inclination)

On this great planet which is our home, we humans have continually striven to discover the nature of our environment and thereby to become more successful in exploiting it. This quest for knowledge has allowed us to become the most intelligent and dominant species, and to gain mastery over all others. The necessity to compete for survival is imposed upon all of nature's creatures, and mankind is no exception. We developed physically and mentally over a great expanse of time, and being inquisitive about ourselves and our surroundings; have investigated and become able to explain the mysterious activities of nature, and the evolution of the species. Consequently, we have found that we are not subject to the whims of heavenly beings wielding supernatural powers, but to the natural conditions that influence our behavior on this planet. This allows us to address our earthly problems in a new light and solve them through our own reasoned efforts. Naturally, we do not know everything and as a result cannot explain everything. However, as intelligent individuals, we must accept the truths of reality as we are able to determine them, and draw conclusions that are in agreement with our observational evidence. The more we learn about the universe of which we are a part the more positively we will be able to act correctly in exploiting it to our advantage.

From recent observations, our astronomers have discovered that other galaxies recede from each other and from ours. Calculating their speed of recession, they have determined that all of the galaxies were once part of a single mass that blew apart about fifteen billion years ago. Our galaxy is an enormous spiral of stars and smaller bodies that rotate and are held in orbit by gravity, it is commonly referred to as the Milky Way. Our solar system, which is located in the outer regions of the galaxy, is believed to have formed from a large cloud of cosmic material which condensed to form our sun and planets about four and one half billion years ago. The planets independently circle our sun and are held in their orbits by gravitational attraction, as is our moon which orbits around the earth.

We cannot at present satisfactorily explain or account for the variations in the motion of the various bodies of the solar system. Their orbital deviations, rotations, and angular momentum do not exactly conform to any mathematical formula that we are able to compound. Finding that there are so many variations, we must admit that we are not aware of all of the factors that were involved in the shaping of our solar system. However, this does not prevent us from attempting to explain the nature of the solar system that is virtually under our feet and which we are continually becoming more knowledgeable about.

Our solar system is composed of varying amounts of the same elements which form our earth. Some of these are radioactive and generate heat as they decay. The heat of kinetic energy in the original formation of our planet, as well as the breakdown of unstable elements since, has caused the earth's centre to achieve and maintain a molten or near molten state. The heavier metallic elements are concentrated in the central core of the earth, and the mantle and outer crust consist mostly of lighter silicate materials. The earth's liquids fill our global depressions and intermingle with the porous materials on the surface. The gases, which the earth's gravity have been able to retain, provide us with the protective atmospheric layers which blanket us from the harmful components of the sun's radiation.

The earth is subjected to gravitational, centrifugal and magnetic forces which have caused its crust to fracture into plates. These separate in areas, making our deep valleys and rifts; and in other areas move toward and over each other to buckle and cause our mountain ranges. The movements of the earth's plates, with respect to each other, are swift and periodic as the stresses become too great. These earthquakes can topple our buildings and injure us, or cause tidal waves at sea. However, we are no longer unreasonably fearful, for the buildup or release of these pressures can now be attributed to natural causes. Only the uninformed and the religiously indoctrinated would continue to accept the unearthly explanations of the spiritualists.

The weathering of the surface of the planet also changes its shape, but in a less dramatic manner. Through time, it has worn down the surface rocks and deposited our soils and sediments; allowing plant life to take root and thrive--transforming the earth's elements into cellulose forms. Plants provided the food material which supported the emergent animal life forms on dry land. Later in time, species evolved which hunted and thrived on the flesh of the plant eaters; and so regulated the numbers of their prey, and in turn were regulated by the scarcity of them. It would appear that all that is necessary is for nature to provide the basic nutrients and a suitable environment. Then organisms thrive and evolve through successfully competing with others for these nutrients.

The diversity of life upon earth and its evolutionary developments are beyond comparison, for we do not have any statistics of happenings upon other similar spheres. This planet appears to have had the proper composition, rotational timing, and temperature ranges for the development of life. The differing species as they exist on earth today, have developed through the natural law of survival of the fittest. Nature provides the foodstuffs for which the various species compete for the necessities of life. The fittest and most adaptable amongst the species survive and reproduce. Environmental circumstances determine the quantities of foodstuffs that nature supplies. All species must suffer the consequences of being regulated in numbers accordingly.

Mankind became the most successful species, overwhelming all others to take command of the resources of the earth. As well as increasing in numbers through taking the provisions of nature that other species relied on, mankind began to assist nature by cultivating, planting, watering, and weeding to increase the production of foodstuffs. We can follow the development of early man's lifestyle by the tools that he shaped or manufactured to aid his cultural endeavors. This transformed our societies as they became increasingly dependent on these practices, from hunters and food-gatherers to workers and producers of the necessities of life.

As man became more dependent upon his agricultural production, it became necessary to protect the area on which he grew his crops or grazed his livestock from the encroachment of others. In this way, he was able to benefit from his toil. Thus as man, or more correctly; as mankind's ancient clans and family groups began laying claim to and defending territory, as well as the assets upon them, they became owners. But in nature's way: ownership is inevitably determined by might, not homesteaders' rights. By overrunning the territories of weaker groups, larger and more technically-advanced groups evolved and became the dominant societies which populated and civilized the earth.

Modern day archaeologists portray our primitive social units as comprising of an assemblage of extended family members, which were held together through kinship, common language, ideology, as well as by the territory that sustained them. As they developed their agricultural techniques they thrived and became less nomadic, and began to erect stronger and more permanent structures for protection from the weather as well as from their enemies. The most successful groups were able to adequately provide themselves with the necessities of life, and to expand their territories; taking over the landholdings of those that were less efficient, and less capable of resisting the aggressor. Historically, the early Greek city-states were typical of an advanced self-sufficient unit. Their people lived within a fortified area for protection, and fought with those who infringed upon their territory or opposed their expansionist activities. Expansion of territorial resources was a definite necessity in order to prevent nature's regulation of them. Consequently, advanced societies continued to increase in population as they captured the territories that supported them–growing in area to become the large national units of our day.

The boundaries of early tribal units were shaped by natural obstructions, and limited in size by the extent of the area over which they could be controlled or defended. As a result, the human species in populating the continents; formed many independent national units, each requiring to protect its territory from those who tried to take it from them. As these units prospered and increased in population, they created a natural pressure at their borders to expand in size, resulting in resistance and warfare where the neighbouring territory was already occupied. This rivalry has plagued mankind, for opposing national groups continue to attempt to capture or exploit additional areas to accommodate the needs of their growing populations. With the development of better and more powerful weapons mankind became more destructive of life and property.

War is the usual and natural outcome of our competitive way of life, and our efforts at making peace will be of no avail as long as we allow this rivalry to continue. Within nations, the citizens have retained their instinctive competitiveness and continue to attempt to gain an advantage over others in their family and social relationships. This is comparable to the pecking order of our barnyards, and portrays our inherent aggressiveness and disrespect for the weak. In our modern societies, these practices have been incorporated in politics by popular demand and have been legalized to become the injustices which are perpetrated under the banner of law and order. Where we have elected or representative government, the minorities must accept the dictates of the majorities or become lawbreakers. Where there is no provision to periodically change the distribution of the political spoils to follow social trends, revolt is common. This is because our majorities demand equality and in most cases an economic advantage. Governments do not produce anything tangible, so they can only partly fulfill the lavish wishes of their political backers. When an immoral majority demands and a political panderer appeases, then the less influential groups, or second-class citizens, suffer economic disadvantages. However, admittedly, we all gain the security of being members of a powerful national unit, and we do benefit from the network of laws which gives us retaliatory protection from other abuses. This security is provided by our law-enforcement agencies and our courts. We have given ourselves most of the property rights that natural conditions do not provide us with, and we have become a cooperative capable of overcoming this natural deficiency within the jurisdiction of our boundaries.

The laws of the democratic nations allow their citizens to own or rent property, from which they attempt to earn their financial requirements. They must pay taxes to their government, which regulates the economy and protects their territorial assets. The government must make rules and enforce laws that contribute to social peace and prosperity, and is expected to administer social justice by catching and punishing those who assault others or deprive them of their personal possessions in an illegal manner. The establishment of individual rights, even though they are not always enforced in absolute fairness, has given industrious societies the security to prosper individually and collectively and to allow their populations to multiply in numbers accordingly. Thus, the need arises within the borders of unregulated societies for larger landholdings and exploitable assets to provide for their increasing requirements. This motivates them and their representatives in government to infringe upon the territorial claims of other nations. Civilized nations have progressed, not through regulating their own numbers in a humane manner, but through overpowering and confiscating the territories of the weaker and less organized. There are no property rights for nations, so they must have their armed forces to safeguard their assets, for might is the determining factor and the strongest prevail.

In primitive times, a group's survival depended upon its ability to remain dominant through maintaining a numerical advantage. As we became industrialized, firepower supplanted manpower; and our survival has become more dependent upon alertness and the economic ability to supply our military forces with an abundance of the most advanced weaponry. As a result of our modern day communication facilities, we have become more knowledgeable regarding national activities on other continents; and with our present transportation abilities, larger numbers of nations have begun to take sides in the contests. We are desirous of defending the type of governmental system and social structure we are familiar with, and are opposed to other religious and political doctrines that diminish the human rights we have grown accustomed to. The development of atomic weaponry has made us face the fact that we cannot continue to compete for survival as we have in the past, for both the victor and the vanquished will surely perish if our wars continue. Our competing societies have developed the ultimate weapon; we can now see where nature's competitive influences are leading us.

In looking back we find that it is the larger social groups that have defeated the smaller clannish groups, and that nature continues to motivate our competitive activities. We are now citizens of a national competitive unit and likely followers of a popular religious doctrine. We are in this position because the only social science that mankind was able to adopt was that which evolved in conjunction with his successes in his struggles for survival. No other social science could evolve, for no other was workable in our competitive environment. Well-reasoned and promoted survival values have been those of the victorious. Less competitive philosophies have failed and their adherents defeated and destroyed. Our societies have been and continue to be locked into a social order similar to that of the ant, for any change would weaken them socially and they would be replaced physically by those that remained most competitive. Consequently, independent societies have been unable to overcome their individual deficiencies or curb their population growth; for any attempt to do so would weaken their nation and make them susceptible to invasion by larger and stronger societies. Civilization has progressed through the cumulative might of those that wisely and faithfully adhered to their survival values, and did not discourage their population increases.

Natural or normal earthly conditions limit our numbers according to that which nature produces or that which humanity can produce from the earth's arable areas. This drives us to compete for these areas so as to earn our needs and the privilege of life. It is and has been common knowledge since ancient times that mankind cannot achieve a peaceful existence as long as we compete for the earth's resources and the produce of others' labors. Lasting peace has been unattainable for war is the natural result of our inability to halt our population increases and aggressions. In order to have peace amongst nations, we must unite: thereby disbanding our competitive groupings, and halt our political practices of taking that which our neighbors have earned. In doing so, we will have evaded the fate that our continuing controversies bring to us, and be able to peacefully produce the provisions for the secure and comfortable life we desire.

Many of course will cling to the superstitions and survival values of our less enlightened eras and pray to their gods to make peace and bring good fortune upon them. However, we must make our own fortune upon this planet by avoiding that which causes our misfortunes. There has been much speculation concerning the existence of an all-powerful and intelligent creator of the universe. We see the stars and we can determine their size and luminosity and are awed by the gigantic forces that created and set them in motion. However, in this advanced age we find nothing to indicate that the powers of the universe are other than that of nature. Therefore, it is most likely that we are not predestined by a greater intelligence, but by our lack of it. We have not been able to understand that the forces of nature cause us to act as we do, and as a result have not been able to escape its control over us. We have allowed natural earthly conditions to keep us competing. In this way, nature rules us. We must overcome the necessity to compete for survival so that we can guide our civilization on a peaceful course.

Ours is not a man-made problem. It has been with us since day one and is the result of the laws of nature. We must recognize that nature is neither our saviour nor our exterminator and apply some rudimentary intelligence to overcome its hold upon us. We are the most intelligent of living creatures and should be capable of overcoming the problems which the ancients could not in less knowledgeable times; so we must by our own initiative, rise above the competitive struggles of the lesser beasts and create the conditions that we desire. Internationally, we must unite all nations under one government in order to prevent wars. Nationally, we must discontinue the political practices of economically disadvantaging minority groups in order to prevent their justifiable unrest and opposition. Individually, we must practice birth control so that there are enough resources so that all can earn their needs and prosper without attempting to gain the assets of others. These should become our new survival values. They are clearly understandable and explained in earthly terms. Only by following this course can we avoid exterminating ourselves and find the peace and contentment that can be ours.

This is a materialistic world and a materialistic life that we lead. We gain our pleasures and satisfactions through fulfilling our physical and sensual needs. We alleviate our pangs of hunger with food that is nourishing and pleasing to our taste. We strive to adequately clothe and shelter ourselves. We desire to participate in the novel and joyous activities of our times, and to have the freedom to acquire property and gadgetry to the extent of our ambitions. We need not restrict our materialistic consumption to accommodate shortages, for we create our own shortages by multiplying the number of consumers. There are only our own needs to be fulfilled to the personal satisfaction of each and every one of us.

During the last century, we have developed adequate transportation and communication facilities to effectively govern the inhabitants of the earth. We are in the process of standardizing our weights and measures to facilitate trade, but we have done nothing and cannot do anything toward developing a common language as long as our nations are opposed and hostile to each other. Our disrespect and mistrust of other ethnic societies has been built up as a result of generations of opposition toward each other. We may be different in our ways and in our spiritual beliefs, but we all have a common desire to gain economic security and to fulfill our bodily requirements and desires while we are here. However, we are all of the same species and are equally deserving of the joys and satisfactions that life can bring. Political and geographical divisions have always separated us, but now, in the interests of universal peace, we must unite the nations and designate a universal language so that we all can conveniently participate in fashioning and operating a government that promotes the equality of the individual, and that brings equal justice to all segments of society, regardless of numbers and past privileges.

The support of individuals is the essential requirement for uniting the species under one government, for only by consensus can the task be accomplished. The majority can always be appeased at the expense of the minority, as is common in the political practices of our day. Yet, with population control, we can satisfy all those that are willing to earn their keep by non-controversial and honorable methods.

Might makes right in nature's scheme of things, and mankind has continued to be governed by might. First, by the might of the family head, and later as we mature; by the practice of governments to mobilize police forces and armies to enforce its bidding. Mankind's great might lies in accumulating greater numbers or a superior force, and then intimidating the remainder to honor its dictates. If political leaders are unsympathetic to the whims of the majority, they then find and support politicians who are willing to appease them. It is not surprising to find that the majority, which is usually composed of influential minority groups, determines the rules controlling our economic purse strings. Before we can perfect our legislation so that it is no longer discriminatory, we must upgrade society's immoral habits, and we can do this by creating the means to satisfy the needs and wants of all. We must fulfill humanity's material needs, not through ever increasing productivity, but through regulating our population so that we attain the necessary resources to adequately provide for our numbers.

Political peace is as important as national peace, and we must refrain from using our beastly might in concert to gain political advantages. Our government must treat all as equals, and must overcome patronage and the controversial practice of bowing to the demands of powerful groups for subsidies and other economic advantages. By eliminating the expectations for favors the greedy rabble will quieten, and dissidents will have nothing of economic consequence to disagree about. Our mores will be based upon reason, rather than spiritual whim and antiquated survival values. Our legal code will become complementary to our moral code, and will amalgamate our present double standard with one set of rules that we can live by and respect. This will create the conditions for the needed stability in government, and allow us to share equally in the rewards of peaceful endeavor. Political peace can only come by outlawing and eliminating the rewards, not by adding fuel to our competitive fires!

In our new world era, the economic burden of defense and aggression will be removed and our taxes can be lessened. The troops will be freed to earn their subsistence from gainful and productive employment. By providing ourselves with a larger workforce, we should be able to reduce our daily working hours. Government will not be intimidated by those that wish to prolong the present status quo; therefore, it will not discriminate amongst its subjects by taxing those that work and are efficient to subsidize those that are unindustrious or inefficient. Many will have to find alternative means of support as we abolish governmental departments and functions. There will be much loss of savings and capital by those that are holding unbacked currencies and other unsecured IOUs, for as our indebited governments become united their former obligations will cease. As well, our governments practice of pyramiding their debts onto larger populations will be reversed as our numbers decline. In reality, the bond-certificates we saved up for a rainy-day may become the handful of paper that we kindle our cookstoves with. But do not despair: for we are now able to correctly identify the forces we are dealing with, and can avoid the catastrophes that they bring upon us.

Through doing that which it is in our power to do correctly, our progress in perfecting conditions upon this planet will give us control of our destiny. As we have already determined the direction in which we wish to proceed, we can pick the safest trail for our journey into the not-so-mysterious future.

If we choose to unite and live in balance with the earthly resources we require to fulfill our needs; we can overcome the need to continue our wasteful and injurious competitions, and be able to create as great a paradise as our intellectual ability can make. It is this life that we wish to make the best, and it is this planet that necessarily must be the field for our new humanitarian science. The earth has the materials and the resources, but only lacks the application of intelligence similar to that which we have applied to our other endeavors; allowing us to rise above the level of the other competitive beasts, as we transcend nature's restrictions and limitations. We will not have achieved eternal life, nor will we gain the necessary provisions for the security of life without effort. Ours will be a man-made heaven, and we the almighty power on earth, will have to earn our keep.

We have done wonders in the fields of medicine, electronics, and in virtually every field that we have explored. We are each of a limited mentality, but as a group have steadily advanced our capabilities. This has been accomplished through passing on our acquired knowledge and experience, which has allowed succeeding generations to improve upon and advance our technologies. But the science of peaceful coexistence, which is promoted here, is not one which has been passed on and improved upon from generation to generation. In fact, it has been stifled so as not to disrupt our society's competitive survival-values and their vain hope of having peace without absolving the need to aggress.

The advance of science brings us much factual information. When Galileo looked through his telescope and determined that the earth was not the centre of the universe as the soothsayers and theologians then professed, he was jailed and forced to recant his findings. The truth could not remain suppressed for long; so books were burned and rewritten to protect our pre-intellectually formulated, and spiritually promoted survival values. The decay of radioactive elements has allowed us to more accurately determine the age of the planet's sedimentary layers and the fossils that we found. This contradicted the chronology of the biblical tale of creation–so the day of creation was lengthened to become an era--thus all was smoothed over until Charles Darwin came along with his theory of evolution. The acceptance of his theory was unpopular with the spiritually indoctrinated societies for it would disrupt their promoted beliefs and survival values. As a result, they declared that the evolution of mankind was not acceptable because of the absence of connective skeletal remains. Despite further archaeological findings, the battle to discredit evolution still rages to this day. However, this suppression of knowledge and the nonacceptance of an accurate description of the forces that govern life on earth, has prevented our societies from understanding and overcoming their competitive affliction.

Our biblical teachings promote uncontrolled population increases, and this density drives us to become more competitive in gaining our sustenance. The pressure to succeed drives us to find easier and better ways to produce our needs: causing us to advance our technology to new heights. These population pressures, as well as creating a need for additional resources; also have advanced our technology toward the development of better weaponry, which makes it easier to infringe upon the resources of other nations. As a result of all this, our natural resources are being depleted, our supporting ecology is being destroyed, and the arms race continues. It's a sad situation that we find ourselves in: being led by the fingers of fate, and being unable to liberate ourselves from its grasp. However, despite being led to believe that we are pawns of heavenly beings, and despite our continued self-destructiveness; I am confident that our acquired knowledge and ingenuity will rescue us from the motivating influences of nature.

Nations whose technical advance was the greatest were able to gain the upper hand and defeat nations in which technical development was slower or lacking. Our past survival values which promoted our planet's population explosion and our technical advances in military hardware have caused us to realize that civilization's progress is toward more and greater conflicts between nations in their interactions to gain or defend territorial assets. We should not continue on this foolish course; and while we cannot and would not wish to halt civilization's technical advances, we must guide ourselves in a manner so as to realize its immediate and long term benefits. This makes it necessary for us to redetermine our survival values and readjust them to make them support our earthly objectives. Therefore, we must counteract the beliefs that contribute to, but fail to alleviate our social strife. We have lately gained the necessary technology, and I endeavor to clearly explain how to avoid our major confrontations.

The progress of civilization has been propelled by the expenditure of human effort in the individual's inherent drive to succeed and find fulfillment in life. The facts, as disclosed by our scientific advancements, cause us to question the rightness of society's actions and can affect our willingness to continue to contribute to a foolish cause. So societies have had to contradict the truths that could weaken them nationally and render them less competitive. It is a case of a little truth confusing us and creating the disunity that threatens our survival. It is only when we have accumulated sufficient truths to guide us on an alternative course that we can accept it and let it be our savior.

We are presently searching the heavens for other intelligences and for additional resources to exploit. We are also driven to advance our space programs for the knowledge and the military advantages they may bring. We do not need more territory to fight over, or someone else to confirm the nature of our problems. We now have the knowledge and the ability to live contentedly on the area we presently occupy, and it is our duty to halt the self-destructive activities we are engaged in. Let us hope that, along with our average intelligence, we have a parental concern for the well-being of the species.

We are able to unite the nations and we have the communication facilities to govern ourselves on our planetary confines. It is high time that we begin to use our heads rather than our brawn: for it is intelligence and not our might which will reduce our need to compete, and allow us to live peacefully while using our available resources to prosper. As we gain confidence in our abilities, and comply with our new survival values, we will be able to prevent the collective destruction of our life support systems and guide our civilization on a desirable course. There is nothing unearthly that stands in our way, so we are free to shape our future as we see fit.

We know that we must prevent the climate of our planet from being changed by protecting the forests that influence our weather patterns and provide us with much of our oxygen. We know that we cannot continue to contaminate our waterways and our oceans as we have in the past without destroying its plant and aquatic life. We have long known that discharge of toxic wastes into the atmosphere causes smog in the cities, acid rain over the countryside, and the thinning of the ozone layer that screens the earth from harmful solar rays. With increasing population there will be more intense competition for the dwindling resources of the earth, and with the ever mounting costs of national and political competition it is not likely that we could find sufficient profits to prevent the destruction of our ecosystems. However, by acting reasonably, we will be able to avoid these unnecessary expenses and be in an improved economic position to prevent further environmental deterioration. This would allow limited numbers to find the means to earn their bodily requirements for incalculable eras. Consequently, it is we that must become the guardians of our earthly assets and intervene to prevent the competitive influences of nature from leading us to our demise.

All I can do is sow the seeds of change, but they must germinate and grow in the fertility of society's mind in order to become fruitful. In other words, our societies must save themselves; there is no other power on earth or in the sky that can do it for us!

Our knowledge of reality has evolved and increased tremendously to supplant the superstitions and myths of our forefathers. We now know that the processes of nature are the effects of natural phenomena. We are no longer overly alarmed by thunder and lightning, or the darkness of eclipses, for we understand what causes them. The magic is explained; the functions of nature become understandable, predictable, and the human species has advanced mentally from the well-wishing of the dark ages to the enlightenment of the twentieth century.

Most of us would like to live in a world of plenty and have everlasting life, but such desires have continued from ancient times and can only be fulfilled by the technology that is available to us. We now understand that God is of our own creation, and desiring such an omnipotent being to do what we cannot do ourselves, does not bring it into existence. Nature can only supply limited and fluctuating quantities, which expanding populations soon decimate; thereby causing competition for these scarcities and resulting in the extinction of the less fit and the survival of the most fit. However, if we were to control our numbers, we could live peacefully and contentedly; not needing to compete for the abundances that we require. Our agricultural techniques increase and provide a more assured production of foodstuffs. Our practices of preserving these to tide us over the seasons could also tide us over many leaner years. We have no alternative but to accept what earthly circumstances provide us with, and make life as enjoyable and long-lasting as possible. We can gain the resources to fulfill our physical needs through the regulation of our numbers. Unwishfully, our bodies tend to wear out and malfunction; we must accept death as the expiration of our physical and mental activities. Our likenesses live on with our children, and with our retirement the young and the inquisitive take their turn in operating our productive enterprises to adequately provide for themselves.

Mankind renews itself as do all other life forms on earth. As well, the cosmos appears to be in a state of change and its elements may in future time provide the material for the rebirth of new stars. Nature appears to control its own, except where control can be wrested from it. So standing here as mortals, and gazing at the heavens, we can only visualize that if we have an intellectual superior, he must be more manipulative of nature than we are in order to do what we cannot do ourselves. However, our knowledge and experiences are with respect to the realities around us. We have no supportive evidence of any life, intellectual or otherwise, beyond the borders of our planet. If the ever-present powers of nature are likened to the heavenly force that the pious claim rules us; I can only say that we are gaining in our ability to evade the damnation of their Lord.

During the last few centuries, with the development of printing, our store of accumulated knowledge has increased tremendously, allowing us to understand and explain the mysterious functions of nature and our ascent from the Stone Age era. At times, we look for evidence that will support our theories, but at other times, the evidence leads us to look elsewhere. We are constantly on the prowl in search of the truth, for most of us are not content to accept the promises of our theologians and politicians.

As the result of our successes in our search for fossil remains, our archaeologists have been able to more accurately determine the various types within related species and the sequence in which they evolved. They have concluded that mankind shares a common ancestor with other members of the primate family. We must admit that early man did not know where he came from, or that the only earthly influence that rewarded or repulsed his efforts was that of nature. Therefore, in this advanced age, we must correct our thinking and our teachings to conform to reality and begin to act accordingly.

As we unravel the mysteries of our past, we gain the ability to see things in a true perspective and can better determine and achieve our objectives in life. Realizing that we are driven by our senses to fulfill our bodily needs as other species are, we should be more concerned about upgrading this life--there is no evidence of another. We would wish to unite the warring nations and steer them from the collision course that they are presently on. We would strive to integrate our economies without creating undue disruption and hardship. We would wish to keep all that is worth keeping, our technical, and industrial capabilities that have eased our burdens; our medical advances that have eased our suffering and prolonged our life span. By reducing our numbers to the level that the earth's limited resources and our fragile ecology can maintain, we would gain the economic security that we require for peaceful and non-competitive coexistence with our fellow man. In this manner, we should be able to progress into an utopian era where we could make further changes for the betterment of mankind as we are able to ascertain them.

These changes would be with respect to the manner in which we govern ourselves. We cannot expect government to give us everything we need on a silver platter without the expenditure of effort on our part. We do not live in a magical world or a spiritual world; we live in a world that is controlled by the forces of nature. Some would like to shift their responsibilities onto others, and demand that the world owes them a living. They demand a welfare cheque large enough to cover their necessities and they continue to cry for more. But government cannot be our god or our slave: it does not produce anything, and should not determine our compassion toward those that are physically or mentally unable to produce. As individuals, we can best determine our own charitable obligations independently; and provide assistance more appropriately, efficiently, and without cause for controversy.

The public purse is the asset of all, and we are all entitled to share equally from the benefits of an all-encompassing authority. However, that authority would have no justification to discriminate amongst us, or to subsidize any specific produce or production. A free marketplace would set the appropriate price for a product. Our administration should not promote a product so as to give its producers an unfair advantage over the producers of another by subsidizing it. Above all, it should not subsidize nonproductivity to the detriment of us all.

Government can only become what we make it. It can only pay out and give benefits somewhat less than it takes in from the taxing and sale of its resource base. However, such benefits as it does provide, should be shared by all; no one should be singled out and treated differently. Government also creates our money and we spend it or save it as we see fit. We can buy any or all of the produce that is on the market and even buy futures on some commodities. We can consume this year's production, but we cannot consume next year's production. However, many have demanded that their representatives in government spend future years' income in order to give themselves benefits that are not available to all and which we cannot provide without borrowing. This practice of deficit spending has given many a false sense that our governments can continue to spend in excess of their revenues. However, the true facts of reality must become more obvious when our debts become so high that we can no longer pay the interest.

The realities of our world are determined by the conditions upon our planet. They are not so harsh that we cannot prosper and find security of life; neither are they so favorable that we can lounge around and live a life of leisure. We must work to earn what we use or consume. When we act correctly with respect to our environment, our efforts are rewarded and we are thankful for nature's help. When we act incorrectly, or fail to act at all, the cupboard remains bare and nature cannot be blamed. So let us use our heads and our hands, otherwise we cannot overcome our deficiencies and provide ourselves with the security we desire.

The following chapters will deal with correcting our im-morality toward our fellow man, and with setting up a government to sustain us as we follow the path toward our earthly utopia. Those who continue to read on will surely come to realize that we are the only intelligence available. No god will aid us, nor will any devil hinder us. Only the powers of nature and our reaction to them need be taken into consideration.

3

The Growth of Knowledge and Technology

(It's our monster and now we must control it)

We have come through the stone age, the bronze age, and the middle ages. We have now progressed to the industrial, electronic, and atomic age. We have been able to increase production as our technologies have advanced. These have allowed our populations to double and redouble a hundred fold.

This population density has also increased our discharges. Our garbage and pollutants have contaminated our rivers, lakes, and oceans. Our rain-forests are being cleared and converted to agricultural production, resulting in a decrease in the amount of oxygen generated. The burning of our coal and petroleum resources has increased the percentage of carbon-dioxide in the air, and contributes to the present global-warming trend. As well, our manufacture and use of hazardous chemicals is claimed to be responsible for the thinning of the atmospheric ozone layer which shields us from harmful rays.

Our ecologists confirm that our activities are destroying our life-support systems. Nevertheless, we do not wish to reject the advances that have modernized our tools and equipment, thus helping us to increase productivity. We strive to improve our nutrition and combat disease, for our technical progress has allowed us to better our standard of living and increase our life-span.

Human civilization progresses as the build-up of knowledge increases, bringing all that is advantageous, but also much that is detrimental to our healthful environment. It would be undesirable, as well as impossible, to halt the advance and use of technology. We cannot stop inventing better methods and equipment. We cannot make the wheels of progress turn backward. The only sensible thing to do is to guide our civilization's progress on a desirable course.

Nature forces all life on earth to be competitive. Mankind has gained the greatest protection from the competition of others of his own kind, by remaining under the protection of a large group or nation. This has given us the safety of numbers in which to advance our technologies, and promote the efficiency of production. It has also allowed us to double our populations and to compete successfully with other rival nations. If we are able to unite the nations this competitive and ecologically destructive course would not need to be continued. By eliminating national competition we would not need large and dense populations which spur the advance of technology and give us the strength to contend with our rivals. In fact, we could avoid the arms race and use the savings to contend with reducing our pollutants and toxic discharges. With the control of our numbers we would be able to live in balance with the resources we require to adequately provide for our needs and could thrive for incalculable generations if we did not destroy our life-supporting ecology.

It is the future of mankind and the organisms that support our species that is being destroyed by the progress of our unguided civilization. By uniting our nations and halting our political discriminations we can gain peace amongst ourselves and overcome the need to promote our ancient survival values that encourage increases in population, and be able to support values that provide for the continuance of future generations. We must guide the course of civilization so as to prevent competition for the earth's real-estate, and show respect for each others equal right to prosper by ending competition at the political level. With adequate resources for all: we would not be driven by shortages of opportunity to exploit each other, and our majorities hopefully would not continue to sponsor laws which gave them an economic advantage over the minorities.

A worthy government cannot discriminate amongst its subjects. It should only provide or oversee the public services we require and desire, and should not be corrupted by the power of the majority and their political representatives to provide economic advantages at the expense of the less influential. With our government not needing to compete with rival nations, it should not redistribute the earnings of the industrious to support the population densities we no longer need or desire. The industrious are the backbone of a society that produces its needs through honest endeavors, and the well-being of our most worthy citizens should be given priority over those that prey or sponge off of them. Politicians and those who have come to live off the efforts of others will have to join the workforce or perish. An honorable and worthy administration cannot subsidize and proliferate the ranks of the lax and inefficient without encouraging the increase of their numbers.

Our societies in supporting methods to overcome the competitive influences that natural circumstances encourage: will wish to unite the nations, control their population numbers, and avoid their social controversies. It will do no good to just unite the nations, and then not control our numbers to gain sufficient resources to overcome our need and motivation to appropriate the earnings and assets of each other. We are driven by our bodily needs and motivations to fulfill them, and we cannot overcome our need to compete against each other unless there are sufficient resources available to give us an alternative. We must provide ourselves with an alternative to our endless wars and political insurrections, for our earthly resources and advancing technologies can be put to better use.

4

As I See it

(The designing of our future)

Our belief in the existence of a beneficial and loving creator has prevented our intelligence from advancing beyond this figurehead. God's domain was that which man could not comprehend, and in enlarging upon these doctrines; our societies have come to amalgamate their survival values with their spiritual beliefs. This has caused the course of human civilization to remain guided by our promotion and adherence to ancient beliefs that remain in opposition to the findings of our modern sciences. The technical advanced societies have outperformed the less advanced, and their methods of using the earth's resources to greater advantage has given the most efficient the power to claim and overrun the territories of the less efficient. The problem remains that mankind is divided into national groups that compete and war amongst each other in order to hold or gain territorial assets. This has locked the course of civilization onto a course that is leading mankind to their competitive demise. We should come to realize that peace and national contentment are unattainable; because of our inability to control our population's aggressive and inconsiderate activities toward other rival nations, and to their own fellow countrymen.

This drive is fueled by shortages of the needed resources which we exploit to fulfill our needs and desires. In order to bring peace and contentment to our species these shortages must be overcome. These shortages are worldwide as well as local, so the remedies to halt our wars and political battles over the division of the earth's resources must encompass all of the national and unclaimed territory on this planet. It is essential to overcome national and political competitiveness as soon as possible; hopefully, before irreparably damaging our environment and exterminating its most mentally-advanced species.

In the past; nations have had to rely on the strength of numbers, and have wisely encouraged population increases. However, the government that we hope to bring into power will absolve the competition between rival nations by uniting them; and by limiting our populations so that there are sufficient resources for all to fulfill their needs. We the people will be the overseers of this government, for we now know the course that we must follow in order to overcome nature's competitive influences. However, we must determine what governmental services we require; and are willing to pay for, before we can arrange for the administration of them.

Individually, we will bring along all that we can carry or afford, and each individual may wish to take a different treasure along. It will not be up to our government to determine what is worthy of keeping. We are all different from each other, and will support the causes or charities of our choice voluntarily. Our government will be a body guided by the intelligence of our citizens, and they will control the course of civilization to the best of their ability to do so. We will probably wish our government to continue to be involved in socialized health care, education, and the management of our monetary and legal systems. Government can perform these tasks as efficiently as anyone. However, when we rely on our government to provide a service, we must ensure the honesty and efficiency of those that are acting on our behalf. The services that we desire of our government necessarily must be payed for. With each individual given sufficient opportunity to become gainfully employed and provide for one's needs as the result of a large reduction in population, the taxes to pay for these services should be levied more equitably upon all that use them.

With population control, parents will not be saddled with more children than they can afford, and the natural drive to prosper and find contentment will encourage these offspring to find a place where they can earn their own way alongside others in a self-supporting society. Our earthly resources must be sufficient to provide the needed opportunities for our population, and our government must discontinue subsidizing anyone or any portion of our society. To do so, would only prolong the political competition and discriminations that are disruptive to peace within a society. Together with eliminating such issues; we also must avoid the costs of deficit spending, which would keep us from reaching our full potential.

The interest we pay on our governmental debts is a burden for which we can only blame ourselves and our politicians. While much benefit has accrued to this generation through going into debt to provide governmental services, and to upgrade our standard of living, the benefit accruing to future generations is small in relation to the debt that has been heaped upon them. There has been no moral incentive in our competitive society to prevent this from happening, and our governments have had to print increasing amounts of money; and resort to inflation, to pay the interest on their debts with devalued currencies. As we watch our debt clock, the numbers keep getting larger as spending continues to exceed revenues. We are now left with no choice, but to take austerity measures to liberate ourselves from the financial quagmire we find ourselves in.

We are a capable species, our basic intelligence and understanding of our problems should allow us to overcome the obstacles that stand before us. We are not magicians, we cannot make water into wine without a few additional ingredients. Neither can we create a utopia without human participation. So I am asking those that live off the efforts of others to cease doing so, and to begin earning their subsistence in an uncontroversial manner.

People may be our greatest asset, as some smooth-talking politicians claim, but a surplus of people will be a great liability toward creating a noncompetitive society. It is likely that we will have to enforce a birthrate of one child per couple until the world's population is reduced to an appropriate level. Then it can be increased to two, when we achieve a balance with the resources we require for contentment.

We will determine what we want and set our goals accordingly. We should not need to be led like sheep; so will not need a leader, but we will need an honest and conscientious administration to formulate and enforce legislation which will guide us on the desired course. Government will be a social project, and the average person's intelligence rather than deceptive politicians should encourage the enactment of legislation to achieve the desired moral standard. We would no longer require the troops and weapons of war, so would wish to eliminate the excessive and undesirable taxes that have been needed to fund the opposing regimes. The manipulation or absolute control of the economy is the source of much of our government's undisclosed income. The inflation rate also has a tendency to devalue our savings and to keep our noses to the grindstone. To regain the full benefits of our toil, we must have complete economic independence! We must recognize this need, and not abandon our chances of gaining political peace by allowing our government to succumb to the demands of the unscrupulous.

Our world government could supply the services that we wished it to provide, but those that supervise them must become accountable to those that pay the bill. We would want to end the violence with which individuals and groups attempt to intimidate each other. However, we would not ask our government to do more than provide the needed protection for the individual: some give and take is necessary in order to determine the proper compensation for wages, services, and trade goods. This give and take should not lead to physical violence, but to the development of safeguards and better business and marketing strategies. The participants in an economy which the government does not control, will naturally lead to justifiable attempts by producers to control prices by limiting the quantities that are put up for sale, and the consumers resisting this price-fixing with their boycotts. Therefore, their should be no grounds for complaint in a marketplace that is free of governmental discrimination and manipulation.

It is to our advantage to be selective, for there are many brands of similar merchandise for sale at the marketplace. This is brought about by competition to fulfill our needs; for there is a lack of opportunity, and the inability of portions of our society to find alternative business ventures. As a result; the prosperity of the manufacturers of duplicate products are dependent upon the public's acceptance of their product, at a price that will provide them with a fair wage. Otherwise, the lack of adequate returns; will force them to accept a substandard wage, or divert to producing a product that provides greater returns. Such economic exploitation is natural, for we all wish the best buy, and consumers are not concerned with the well-being of the producers of the products that they select. Naturally, we are more concerned about our own well-being than we are over that of our suppliers.

In order to be successful, manufacturers must keep abreast of the latest technology and avoid turning out a product that has become obsolete or overpriced. However, we cannot all become successful in manufacturing the same product, people must have sufficient opportunities to earn their livelihood by alternative means. As a whole, they must sell enough to buy what they want from others, and stay reasonably efficient in their production, but they do not need to let the consumer have all the say at the marketplace. The producers of a product will wish to have a comparable living standard to those gained in other industries and occupations, so must be able to control the quantity that is put up for sale in order to achieve this.

The free marketplace is where the demand for a product meets the quantity of production, and determines its present value. The price of a product that is in oversupply will deteriorate, and not provide a comparable wage to its producers. This can be corrected by reducing production until scarcities influence higher prices. In a reverse situation, where prices and profits are high; production will be increased until the shortage is met, and prices and profits return to a lower level. However, the economy in most countries is in the hands of governments which attempt to keep it buoyant to provide opportunities and jobs for increasing populations, and in doing so; provide themselves with an expanding tax base to fund defense and aggression. The average person has had little experience in controlling their own economy, which is in the hands of devious politicians, or the economy of a nation. However, a wise society will not desire an economy that is regulated by politicians who use it to safeguard their own positions by bribing the voters. Neither are they likely to want a socialist type of control: where prices and wages are set by the bureaucracy, and the incentive to be productive and efficient is lacking–resulting in a lower standard of living for everyone.

A world administration should have no cause or motivation that is not considered by the public to be to the benefit of all. Neither should it borrow and cause the inflation rate to spiral, or to tax the economy to slow it down. Our society should be able to easily provide for the peacetime public services it requires, and there could be no moral justification for a society to pawn off this expense upon those that earn the most or work the hardest. It is the individual's economy that we should be concerned with; and I am satisfied that the economic pie, or the payments for our efforts, can best be apportioned by the marketplace. There will definitely be no paydays for those who do not produce anything, and have nothing to sell.

It is not a desirous function for our government to dictate our individual worth, or to arbitrate in our economic disputes with those we may work for, but it should enforce the legislation that the ruling majorities may desire to promote safe working conditions for those that work for others. It is the individual whose numbers form the populace, and it is for the individual that we require government to enforce the rules that we agree to live and play by. It is our happiness and prosperity that is at stake--our government should be no more than the tool to bring order among us, and administrate the common requirements for an advanced society--leaving individuals free to reach their own economic goals, and to determine how high on the hog they will eat. For example: we will desire roads, law enforcement, educational, and hospitalization facilities; communication, and transportation networks; utilities, money and trustworthy institutions for handling its manufacture, distribution, and storage. Some of these tasks we will administer by consigning them to governmental departments; we may leave others for private enterprise. Our public services should be in the hands of employees that are proficient in their duties, and their activities should be overseen by a watchful public. There will be no need for elections as there will be no political discrimination allowed, and no gifts to appease the majorities. As a consequence, we will appoint our governmental employees for their superior abilities; academic tests should suffice. Some of us will earn our subsistence from governmental employment, and the demands upon our time and our wages should be comparable to those in the private sector. Our employees should be accountable for their actions, as we all are expected to be, and should not be free to bribe us with our own money or to aggrandize themselves at our expense.

We know that competent administrators are necessary for good government, but administrators are human, and can be as corrupt as any of us. Therefore, it is the public that must keep them honest by constantly looking over their shoulders and monitoring their activities. Our governmental supervisors will be picked from among us, and we hope to choose the most brilliant and dedicated. They will work for us and oversee the governmental departments to maintain acceptable standards and procedures, and to promote efficiency; for we should not be so foolish as to support and create a class better than our own. We must allow our supervisors to set the wage scales for the civil service; preferably at a level that neither results in an excess or shortage of qualified applicants for the positions. We may also allow them to set their own wages within reason, but by no means will we allow them to set our wages or deprive us of our earnings in the private sector.

Civil servants and public works employees have been partly insulated from the stresses of competition. Their departments or Crown Corporations need not generate a profit, and efficiency has consequently deteriorated. The extra expense does not come out of their manager's pockets, so they can easily overlook their employee's infractions. Job security is unparalleled and a governmental employee's usual incentive is to climb up the administrative ladder to higher paying positions. Private contractors are usually able to perform many of the government's periodic chores at a lesser cost, and still make considerable profits. They must remain efficient by maintaining their equipment in good repair, and must send their careless and lax employees down the road.

In the civil service the supervisory staff and the workers are in the same boat, and since lax employees are rarely weeded out; the public gets stuck with the cost of supplying extra employees and equipment to do the work. We cannot hire more civil servants to oversee the efficiency of other civil servants–the public must monitor and rate its own employees. There is no need, nor should there be a desire, to provide greater job security or pensions for those that are hired to work for the government than in the private sector. Everyone should be equally obligated, and encouraged by fair economic conditions to expend the energy to earn their groceries. None should be cushioned at the taxpayer's expense.

When the public comes to realize that they are being influenced by the powers of nature to continue on an undesirable and competitive course, they will surely take the necessary action to free themselves from nature's damnable hold upon them. They must unite the nations and fashion a world government that respects the rights of all. Our government cannot favor any portion of society, or discriminate amongst its subjects, for it would then provide motives for its overthrow. It is only by limiting our numbers and providing sufficient opportunities for all: that we can fulfill our needs and hope to prevent an immoral majority from demanding economic advantages--it is this contentiousness that we must avoid! Our government must remain neutral and uncorrupted. A wise and farsighted species must promote the ethics to fashion and keep it that way.

Industry and labor have been continuously at odds over wages, working conditions, and other off duty gratuities, but government cannot be the referee. With no interference or protection from government, it is likely that workers will join with management and become shareholders in their ventures; thus sharing in the profits of their own productivity. As a result, most large producers will likely become little socialist organizations; all working for the good of the unit and benefiting accordingly. They will likely have their own medical and group pension plans. Those that benefit, will be those that worked and earned; and it is not likely that those that do not participate will get anything for free. However, there is corruption and graft most everywhere one looks. Cooperative ventures in agricultural production and shareholders in companies that produce other products must monitor their managers and their manager's side-kicks more closely. They should not be given the freedom to use their position to monetary advantage, or to give themselves wages and perks that are greatly in excess of that given to other workers. No one can be expected to be more fair or more honest than they are forced to be.

We will continue to advance our industrial and technical abilities, and will desire the items that we are accustomed to having, as well as the new items that our advancing technology makes available. These items will be manufactured by groups that have elected to earn their subsistence in that manner, and they will expect to earn comparable wages to those in other sectors. The public's demand for these goods will determine their worth, and where monopolies and unrealistic pricing occurs; the public will be free to set up competitive sources of supply. Tariffs, protective and anti-dumping legislation will be abolished; for trade will be conducted on a worldwide basis. There will be no special legislation for favored groups, because there should be no government pets. With input from an alert citizenry, and their awakened sense of morality; our legislation should lose its offensiveness, and our rules will become acceptable. However; if majorities continue to impose their will upon government to give themselves unfair economic advantages, our civilization will definitely retain its opposing and self-destructive course! Majorities must not let their greed and presumed greater need corrupt the integrity of government, for we can create the opportunity to fulfill our needs without competing at the legislative level. In the past, societies were not able to understand what caused them to continually bicker over the division of the spoils. We must stop fighting over the real estate and the profits of our neighbor's toil if we are to avoid our fate. We individually, or as a group, have the power to physically compete to gain an economic advantage. Therefore, we must teach each other that these beastly activities are not morally correct; and should not be permissible, or necessary for survival when earthly resources become plentiful as the result of the regulation of our numbers.

As civilization progressed and nations became more densely populated; their citizens specialized in various trades and bartered amongst themselves, as well as exported to other nations. Durable items that were not perishable, and small in relation to their value; became the most popular medium of exchange, for they could be easily transported or concealed. Coins made from rare metals became most widely used because they could be sized to achieve different values. They served the needs of early man quite well, but as they wore down they became lighter and less valuable. In time each nation or economic unit took it upon itself to issue legal tender to the exclusion of all others. At times the gold or silver was diluted with base metals, and in later times paper notes were issued to represent gold and silver in storage. However, being on a gold standard imposed too great a monetary discipline upon our politicians and representatives in government. In times of war there was need for increased manufacture of weapons and in times of recession it was desirable to stimulate the economy to increase employment. Of late, most countries have circulated far more currency than the worth of gold they have in storage and have borrowed heavily from each other, and from their own citizens. This failure of our representatives to curb their spending, has required that larger portions of the tax revenue be spent on paying interest on the debt; and since we and our politicians seem unable to balance our budgets, conditions can only become tragic as we sink into debt beyond our ability to recover. In the past there have been many instances of a near or total collapse of a nation's monetary system; and in such instances, it is common practice for a nation to recall its old bank-notes and issue new ones at a high premium. This results in extremely high inflation, but this is preferable to allowing an economic structure to collapse. In this way, our governmental debts are reduced and passed on from generation to generation. Our world banking system is also in trouble, for it has partially abandoned the gold standard and trade between nations is conducted largely through the use of credit.

With population under control, we will have no need to increase the amount of money in circulation; and while we need not revert to a gold standard, we need to maintain monetary stability and fiscal responsibility. We all wish to be able to exchange our money for things we need or want; and as long as we do not devalue our money by increasing its quantity, there should be no fear of holding it in preference to other things of value.

Gold and other rare metals are presently being mined to create a profit for the mining companies. With the demand for rare metals being reduced, as a result of having a stable monetary system, the value of these metals will be dependent upon the industries that use them for other purposes--any surplus production would flood the market and drive prices down. It is simpler to regulate the amount of currency in circulation, and let the marketplace determine the value of all the other commodities according to their availability. We must allow the loaning of money to earn interest, or the selling of assets on credit by individuals or companies to drum up trade. We all wish to have the freedom to use our assets to advantage or to even give them away. These practices redistribute our buying power or our produce, but they do not cause inflation as does the creation of IOU's and credit documents that do not have the security of an equivalent worth of commodity on hand.

Governments and the general public have both grown accustomed to spending their next pay-cheque before they get it. It has become legal and acceptable for financial institutions to make loans and draw interest, using fractional reserves as security. They also are the main issuer of credit-cards, which increases the public's ability to purchase scarce commodities and drive prices upwards. These also give some people more credit than they are able to manage, resulting in extremely high interest payments charged to those that default on their monthly payments. Mining companies, as well as other producers hedge the price of their anticipated production on the futures market and gain cash or access to credit ahead of time. These practices increase the public's buying power and contribute to inflation; the same as if the government issued additional script.

Our government should remain in control of the value of the dollar, and we should not allow anyone to counterfeit it, or debase it in any manner. With a stable population, we will never need more or less currency in circulation. Our money or monetary units will derive a variable value of exchange, and will become more or less valuable in relation to other commodities as circumstances dictate. However, it should not continually lose value through the issuance of excessive amounts of government money or through allowing non-governmental parties to float their paper.

There are many types of credit instruments, and some perhaps that have not yet been invented. Therefore, we must discourage all types of credit promotions that increase the public's buying power. Our laws must have a designated purpose, and be designed so that they do not exclude those that are determined to make detours around our no-trespassing signs. I am of the opinion that if our government refused to enforce the collection of IOU,s that infringed upon its monetary control, they would fall into disuse.

At present, an increase in the amount of money or credit available allows our societies to speedily expand production of highly profitable items, and to meet the emergencies of war. With our wars eliminated, and our population numbers in check, we will be able to avoid inflation by keeping our buying power at a uniform level.

With control of population densities: our offspring would less likely be driven out of their homes, and the area of their upbringing due to overcrowding, and would be in line to inherit the productive enterprises of their parents and sponsors. Furthermore, there would be no distant continents to colonize, no greater opportunities elsewhere to inspire migration. Government would not be a party to unrestrained social programs that would increase our indebtedness or raise our taxes. The surplus capital (which is the savings of the people) would be used exclusively by the private sector to modernize and upgrade their productive facilities.

After replacing national currencies with a single international currency the control of its supply would enable us to bring inflation down to zero. Thereby creating stability and the necessary confidence in our currency that our previously-unsupported monetary systems did not generate. In manufacturing, where the cost is divided between material and labor, the yearly battle over wages would cease. The price fluctuations of a product would likely remain within a narrow range until technology introduced an improved product, or an easier method of manufacture. The fluctuation of prices between manufacturer and consumer would be stable for longer periods, allowing better comparative shopping and budgeting. Also, this stability would allow us to better choose a vocation, for the rewards would become more closely tied to the tediousness of the job.

In agriculture, where the weather plays a large part in determining quantities, the rule of supply and demand would also apply. Marketing boards and other price fixing agencies would no longer have government support. However, agreements amongst producers would not be prevented; because of the necessity to limit the quantities that are for sale, to safeguard prices and profits. Therefore, the scope of price setting or gouging would only be limited by the laws that would protect individuals and their private property. If a regional area overpriced its product, or if it could be produced more cheaply elsewhere, then the transportation of goods would be economically justified. Government must consider both the producer and the consumer, and having done so would not be justified in wronging either party in an attempt to make right. Therefore, our government should not be at the bargaining table, for it would have nothing to sell.

Presently, governments negotiate with each other to set the trading price of grains, oil, etc, and to establish quotas and tariffs so as to protect their own producers from the exploitative practices and low wages of other countries. Because of this the international market has not been a free market where the principles of supply and demand establish prices, or in which trade can take place without the approval and protection of governments. In the future, with no controversial foreign powers on the scene, individuals and groups would be able to trade worldwide, and the price of commodities should not differ much over the cost of transportation from one locale to another. We would all be subject to the same economy and level of prosperity, for trade would be unrestricted and there would be no quotas, tariffs, or excise taxes imposed by our government–there would be no reason to have them.

Those involved would control the quantities that they market and would be responsible for their own prosperity. They would also become responsible again for their personal needs, for our government would not be in the business of supplying these to them. Under our present quasi-capitalism, we have direct sponsorship through welfare and government-controlled and subsidized pensions and medical care; all of which is payed for by the taxpayer. We can expect this type of income equalization under a socialist regime where all work for the state. In our new system of free enterprise, we would no longer be working for the government. Therefore, we should not expect our government to set our wages or supply our basic needs. Our citizens should not be free to help themselves to the benefits of others' labors by demanding a continuance of governmental redistributions and equalization payments. They must learn to pay their own admission, thereby avoiding the controversy and strife of a welfare state that our government has not been able to effectively police and administer.

We would need a local municipal type of administration to provide titles to the holders of fixed assets and to oversee education, hospitalization, roads, law enforcement, and so on. I cannot determine, at this time, what portions could be best provided by private enterprise or contractual arrangements; but I am sure that the citizens of the future will determine what is best for themselves.

Our contact with government would be greater at the municipal level, and the opportunity for discrimination and administrative corruption would definitely be greater where money is involved. There would be the assessment of property for taxation in order to finance public services, licenses, and fuel taxes for those that use our transportation facilities. We also would need a head tax to provide the revenue for our central government. We cannot justify discrimination through taxation, so we would likely discontinue income taxes, inheritance and gift taxes, and other taxes that are directed at the most industrious or those with the ability to pay. It is our children, and not the government that should receive our inheritance. In this way a stable productive operation would not be penalized and become less viable as a result of a death. However, with respect to the taxation of alcohol, drugs and other degenerative products; we would have to make an exception and tax them, in order to compensate for the disruptions that their use causes within a society.

To tax alcohol and drugs in a world of plenty would only discriminate. Taxation will not curtail their use. The only way we can protect the public is through education. To ban or regulate the sale of such substances infringes upon our freedoms and usually leads to criminal activities. Freedom to use these impairing and habit-forming products would affect the ability of many to also feed and shelter themselves--creating beggars and desperados. Therefore, these products should be taxed to bring in sufficient funds to provide for extra policing. The well-being of the individual is the concern of all, but the maintenance of our health and economic viability is our own personal responsibility.

The public at large should not be taxed to support a class of paupers, however they may come into being.

Present governments, with the approval of the majority; tax, regulate, or attempt to ban tobacco, alcohol, and other addictive and degenerative drugs. Most of us are aware of the sad consequences of banning the sale of alcohol in the USA during the prohibition years. Nowadays we are experiencing a similar problem. The profits from producing and distributing illegal drugs provides lucrative revenue for organized crime. The high price of these illegal and euphoric substances motivates the users to resort to many illegal activities that provide highly profitable returns. Also, our present regimes are notorious for dishing out the earnings of the law-abiding to subsidize those that are able to hide their ill-gotten-gains. Therefore, all government giveaways must be terminated in order to eliminate the continuance of such scams. Our government must become an institution that strives to provide benefits to all, and to prejudice none. Friends, acquaintances, and relatives are concerned over the plight of those that don't make the grade. They are inclined to give them helpful advice, or to even assist them financially. Society and its administration, as a whole; does not share these same personal relationships, and should not allow the expenditure of public funds for private purposes. They should be mostly concerned about providing the beneficial public services that an able-bodied species can afford and is willing to pay for. Individually, we can all give our surpluses away to charitable concerns, but we first must give priority to our own needs. Nature no longer supplies our increased requirements so we must earn sufficient for our needs with the expenditure of effort. There are some that habitually and persistently prey upon those that earn, so we must remove the morally deficient from our presence in order to protect ourselves.

It is understandable that we must have laws to encourage peaceful coexistence. Our society and its government must enforce these laws, and thereby discriminate between the law-breakers and the law-abiding. Our society will surely abandon its coddling of capital offenders as it overcomes its spiritual restraints over the sanctity of life. The punishment must more closely fit the enormity of the crime. For lesser offenses, there are many island locations where the disobedient could be easily and economically segregated. There are also many productive activities that would reintroduce the offenders to the physical and mental labors that are needed to earn an honest living. This is not and cannot be construed as cruel and unusual punishment. Even the well-behaved are subjected to the need to be industrious in this advanced era. We should not be giving out free room and board to anyone; and in particular to those who unrightfully take or steal the assets of others. They are no different than the wolf within the flock, or the leach that feeds on the lifeblood of its victim. By not freeing the criminally inclined from the need to earn their keep, they may in time be willing to rejoin us in the free world where work hours are not so compulsory.

It should be the government's responsibility to provide us with the opportunity to earn to the extent of our ambitions, and not to tax us unjustly for having done so. However, it is not the government's business to say how we should spend our earnings in our attempts to find happiness. I do not believe that it is desirable for government to legislate individuals into submission or conformity. But, in a world in which we must earn the necessities of life and our standard of living through toil, this must be our first priority before we are free to play.

It is not likely that our rules will be perfect at the outset, for all we can do is make rules to the best of our ability. An enlightened society will demand that our laws prevent all discrimination, rather than continue to be the instrument by which we have been defrauding each other of economic equality. We will wish to bring rival and opposing factions together, and will need to eliminate the use of all discriminative legislation in order to overcome the political dissension amongst us. So, for rules that are below the level of our intellect, and for rules that have been designed for other purposes: let them be preserved in history to remind us of our follies.

In our early eras, nature kept the species physically and mentally fit, but as mankind became the most dominant and continued to develop better agricultural methods, there was nothing to regulate him and keep him in top condition. However, we no longer need to be keen of eye and fleet of foot to flourish. We only need to perform the tasks that provide us with our daily needs. Therefore, with our government neither financially supporting the able or the disabled, our citizens will retain the needed capability to prosper by their own initiatives. We have but to determine and enforce the needed legislation so that we can rise above the combativeness of the other beasts and achieve the prosperity that we are capable of.

It is more essential that the able save themselves than be mired down in their attempts to accommodate the shiftless, the fraudulent and the infirm. Charity begins with the individual: from the heart of the donor. Our leniency does not come from the heart when we are taxed. Let us give as we see fit and let those that bleed for others do likewise. In the recent past every family had the responsibility to look after its own charitable cases, but with disability, medical coverage, and pension insurance; those that are willing to pay the premiums could provide themselves with the protection they can afford--their earnings would not be taxed to provide similar governmental programs.

The reason why we must relieve our government of financing and operating our present social assistance programs is that these are not the survival values that it should promote. It cannot be the keeper of those that do not have the ability to earn their keep, for it is kept by those that are able to do so. Our new government cannot continue to subsidize one segment of society without indebting and offending the other. Our individual survival is dependent upon our ability to exploit our earthly resources, and humanity's prosperity is dependent upon regulating its numbers so that there are sufficient resources for its needs. The charitable causes that these self-sufficient individuals contribute to is not a governmental concern, and our new government should not become involved in how well individuals choose to provide for themselves and their dependents. Its prime purpose is to enforce the legislation that will effectively lead our species toward peace and plenty, while managing the public services we desire and are willing to pay for.

Medical, disability, and retirement coverage could best be supplied by nongovernmental institutions, but again by those that are willing to pay the premiums. It is unclear to me how far we should get involved in regulating insurance and banking institutions so that they do not default on their commitments. We will probably have to rely on those with greater knowledge and experience in these fields to aid us in these matters.

Individually, we must keep mentally and physically fit to perform the essential tasks to gain the necessities of life. It will be easier for those who are healthy and energetic, but there is no reason why those less agile cannot participate in earning their own keep and in enjoying the rewards of life. Government will not determine the fitness level, but circumstances and one's ability to acquire the necessities of life will. We will have no reason to raise mental or physical invalids who may become too great of a financial burden upon us, nor will we wish to have laws preventing us from dealing with our own defective reproductions in a practical manner.

With advanced methods, we are more able to determine the health of the fetus during the gestation period and could terminate the pregnancies then. Other defects result from physical injuries and exposure to harmful substances during gestation. Some result in miscarriages; others will have to be evaluated as their abnormalities become apparent, but we will be responsible for providing for our own charitable cases if we have the inclination to further their existence. No one should be taxed to pay the cost of someone else's personal concerns. Medically, we will also have to limit our expenditures upon ourselves and our dependents to the level of our ability to pay for transplants and other life-sustaining devices. Medical technology is virtually free and readily available to those that choose to follow this profession, but we should not expect the public to bear the expense of hiring doctors to remedy the ailments of private citizens.

Knowledge of reliable birth control methods will be advantageous to humanely restrict our numbers. There are a number of practical methods for the prevention of pregnancy and we can resort to sterilization when we have begotten our quota of children. Also, as a last resort, we have abortion. With these methods we should be able to please everyone except those that are determined to disrupt the process of regulation.

Education should be designed to create responsible citizens: attentive to the need to prevent dissension within our singular society, and to be respectful of the equal rights of others while they exploit the abundant resources of our planet. We will be teaching reality as we have found it to be, rather than spiritual beliefs that tend to increase our competitive numbers, thereby preventing the proliferation of the misinformed and the sucker that is theoretically born every minute. We cannot legislate excessively and treat our subjects as children, but we can educate them and attempt to make them equally intelligent as they mature. However, we will all have to come to understand that our civilization progresses in a forward direction. We cannot abandon the technology that increases our efficiency and raises our productivity and living standards. None can revert back to living on the meager provisions that nature provides, for our prosperity is enhanced by how well we assist nature in increasing the provisions we require and desire.

Our laws and our moral standards will support each other for they will be one and the same. That which is legal will become moral, and what is moral will be supported by our new legislation. We should not be burdening our children with our deficit spending, thereby not exploiting them before they are born. Likewise, we should not allow them to enter into legally binding business contracts until they are of age, so as to prevent them from being exploited before they are educated. We would also wish our children to have the opportunity to find success in their endeavors and to find contentment in life. It is our responsibility as parents to raise offspring that are physically and mentally capable of coping with reality. Our laws would assist us in achieving these objectives and should discourage excessive exploitation of children until they reach maturity. Parents however, have a duty to teach their offspring to accept our methods of producing our needs through toil. They can best do this by assigning light tasks to their children so that as they mature they will become accustomed to sharing the work with their elders, and fit in with others that produce their necessities through a fair exchange of labor.

Our sexual lifestyle is determined by our environment and the opportunities that it offers us. Individually, we follow our own preferences within limits imposed upon us by social, physical, and economic conditions. Consequently, the sexual freedom of individuals has varied as our family groups have changed. However, our survival has most always been dependent upon us providing for our offspring until they are mentally and physically able to look after themselves. So in that sense, our unrestrained sexual freedom will be limited to the extent that the parties involved provide the needed support to their offspring.

The family group of the future will reflect our social needs and our sexual desires. Differing types of family units will evolve and endure to the extent that they are stable enough to carry themselves forward from generation to generation. They will vary from single couples to multiple unities, and the populace as a whole, should have no reason to frown upon those that band together to better utilize farming machinery, or who resort to extended family housing to better care for the elderly, and also to oversee and teach the social amenities to their youngsters. While these arrangements provide the opportunities for greater economic fulfillment, they also throw people together into relationships which may lead to a widening of our sexual tolerances.

One of our present survival values has been to promote heterosexual contracts between men and women, so as to provide for a greater parental presence for the rearing of the young. This has limited our sexual freedom and has led to much adultery and abuse. Our national security will no longer be dependent upon the might of numbers, so our new government should no longer discriminate amongst sexual practices, and no one should be subsidized to defray the cost of child rearing. Those that have desirable personal relationships will stay united to reproduce and support their youngsters. This will bring us larger numbers of households that exist as the result of lifestyles that are favored and which should become more socially acceptable as we overcome our dogmatic repressions.

Our children mature much slower than other species and must be cared for much longer as a result. We no longer subsist exclusively on the provisions of nature, so must learn to produce our needs through exploiting our resources. We must educate our children to use techniques by which to earn their livelihood in competition with others in our industrious society. This requires prolonged parental support, but it does not require that we practice any particular sexual code. We wish to regain the sexual freedom that other species have continued to enjoy, and develop the relationships that satisfy both our economic and sensual needs. Our government should not be asked to recognize any particular sexual arrangement, or to choose between the practices of different racial groups--all must be free to practice their accustomed or desired lifestyles.

If we expect to be free, we must respect the equal rights and freedom of others. There are instances when our freedoms should be curtailed, but I am confident that they will be outlawed and enforced indiscriminately. Our moral and legal codes will make individual men and women equally responsible for limiting the numbers of, and providing for their child or children. Children will be conceived with the full awareness of the consequences of our lovemaking. Therefore, children will be conceived in the eyes of man and should not be faulted through not having been conceived within the spiritual unions and acceptable family groupings of our various societies.

As well, as overcoming our present sexual repressions, we will become members of a society with sensible and realistic objectives. We will not have the freedom to propagate to excess and compete numerically. Neither will we need or desire to propagate in excess of the opportunities that our environment, and our manipulation of it provides. Our family structure will reflect our individual choices, not those of our past social dictates. There is only one cause and that is our own. We need not and should not take anything else into consideration, for to do so would cause humanity's needs to become secondary.

We are the recipients as well as the perpetrators of our fortunes upon this planet. We have come to recognize our problems and can avoid our progression towards self-destruction, and could enter into an era where there would be sufficient opportunity to satisfy our industriousness. With freedom from excessive and unwarranted taxation we would gain the desired and required level of economic security. Therefore, in the future, our days of rest would be of our own choosing and as plentiful as our individual efficiencies and economic conditions would allow. We would not be assets and objects for administrative manipulation, so we would not desire to be told when or when not to work. We would make hay when the sun shone, and lie in the shade when we had enough money in the bank. Our energy being our own, we would expend it as and when we pleased. We would retire or semi-retire as our own personal economic conditions warranted, and we would be free to postpone this period indefinitely if we so desired. Our belated retirement would not deprive the younger generation of employment or of becoming self-employed; because, with population control, there would be sufficient opportunity for all.

We will not have much need for guns in a world of plenty. Yet, we must be willing to protect that which is ours. In rural areas, we would likely live further from other family groups and from the protection of police than we do now. We need protection before the fact as much as we need the involvement of law enforcement after the act. Within the family unit, the use of force and the abuse of the weaker sex by the stronger is not justified. We are the mightiest of all the species but our might comes not through brawn but through the intelligent application of tools and weapons. Therefore, let none take advantage of our sociable nature, for physical might does not make right.

A weapon in our home would make it a woman's castle also, thereby, preventing the abuse of the weaker sex as much as it would discourage dominance by the stronger. I do not profess to begin a war between the sexes, but since we have the technology for weapons of mass destruction, let us develop relationships in the presence of weapons so that we can develop relationships of equality and mutual respect. Our objective should be to remain in control of our own personal lives. We are more capable of protecting ourselves than are those we can hire to penalize the assailants and lawbreakers afterwards.[1] Weapons are an equalizer, but there are those that do not believe in equality. They are those that are most likely to abuse us. Therefore, we should not need to use conventional weaponry except to protect ourselves from those that persistently assault us in taking advantage of our physical weaknesses.

With intelligent application we harness the power of the universe, the power of electricity and electronics, the power of our fossil fuels, and the power of the atom. Along with this power we must develop the responsibility to use it wisely and constructively. We do not wish to ban anything the populace may desire or require. By amalgamating the rival nations we would be creating the peaceful conditions where we would not need to use atomic weaponry. By outlawing political competition and discrimination we create the conditions where we could live with less animosity and in greater harmony with each other.

We should not attempting to disarm or reduce the might of the individual, but we must create favorable conditions for an industrious species to find the needed opportunities for fulfillment in life. Those that are not able to do so within the law, and by their own initiative, are not fit to further their own kind. They will naturally die out as they should, leaving us with a more conscientious and responsible populace to carry on with the task of maintaining the peace by preventing the confrontations that naturally occur as the result of the limited resources of our planet. However, conditions will not be perfected overnight, and until there is a substantial reduction in population to provide increased per capita opportunities, there will be shortages and

1. A police officer may be reluctant to charge a lawbreaker who is an acquaintance, or a friend of a friend. They can be as discriminatory as anyone, and there is only the chief to complain to. Also, when criminals distance themselves from the area of the crime, the cost of apprehending and returning the party for a hearing will have a bearing on how well our laws are enforced.

In cases of cheques that are NSF, I have found that the size of the cheque and the disposition of the officer complained to may determine whether a charge is laid. I have also encountered discrimination by our police forces in refusing to enforce the law equally upon some minority groups, who have a number of reasons to reject our society's modern methods and rules, and are already the major inhabitants in our Canadian jails. Therefore, one would be wise to protect one's person and property more effectively and rely less upon third-parties and tribunes that may fail to do so.

probably a proportionate incidence of crime. So the forces of law and order can only be diminished as harmony increases, and the motivation for crime fades away.

We are producers as well as consumers. Our standard of living would depend upon our ability to produce and we should be content to live within our means. Therefore, we should not partake of the forbidden fruit by deceit or force, for it is the produce of our neighbor.

We are not born wise, but we are born with the ability to learn. We should learn how to live contentedly on the ample resources that we have to exploit. Our parents and schools should teach us to respect the rights of our fellow man. As we grow up, we will strain at the bounds imposed by our parents and society. Our experiences will instill in us a sense of morality, which will be further supported by our laws and law- enforcement agencies. We will become wise as we mature, but all of us will not become model citizens. Some of us will have had poorer teachers or be more stubborn and slower to learn than others.

Crimes are committed for various reasons, but they are all injurious to the victim. Our names are different, but our offenses have all been categorized. Therefore, we must standardize the penalties that are imposed upon the offenders to provide equal justice to all. The political pressure upon our judicial appointees would be eliminated, but social influences will remain. If the penalties that are allowed to be imposed upon the convicted are reduced to a narrow range, there will be less discrimination and opportunity for graft. We should desire greater equality in our courts, and would be offended if we were singled out and treated more harshly than others. The freedom to corrupt and confound the law has been too great, but we would become more equal when we prevent the discriminations of our law-enforcers and attune our new world government toward desired and acceptable standards.[2]

Economically, we would all retain such possessions as we now have. In instances of joint ownership and mortgaged assets, the percentages would be retained accordingly. I suspect that virtually every agreement made by present governments would be voided with the exception of material assets and possessions. Native and aboriginal people would have to accept the productive ways of our advancing civilization. With reduced populations, there would be enough resources for all those that have the energy to exploit them. No one would continue to be pampered at public expense, nor would anyone be deprived of equality when we develop a society that respects the ideals expressed here and allows us to entrench these rights in our constitution.

We have all become subjected to the industrious ways of our advanced civilization—some more recently than others. Its superior productivity has superseded the stone-age practices of scrounging for the scarce and undependable provisions of

2. We have many laws that are regularly being enforced, but also many that are obsolete and rarely enforced. Our law-makers have been so busy updating new laws that they have neglected to rescind the old. These old laws can be enforced at the discretion of our law-enforcers—it is for this reason that we must update our law-books and reduce discrimination by narrowing the range of the penalties that can be imposed upon the convicted.

In Canada, we have "The Young Offenders Act." Juveniles may or may not be elevated to adult court, and penalized more harshly as adults are. It seems to depend upon who you are, and what political connections you have. Young offenders probably should not be shielded when they commit capital crimes, but until this becomes the law we should not discriminate amongst them.

When the establishment throws the book at you in one instance or out of the window in another, it is usually the result of politicians interfering to gain popularity with their constituents and supporters. This corrupts the enforcement of our criminal laws, while other politically sponsored laws manipulate the economy of law-abiding citizens. We must prevent our future administration from meddling in these matters, for a government cannot play favorites and remain above reproach.

nature. We have learned how to provide for ourselves more adequately, and in using modern agricultural methods and equipment have increased our per capita production tremendously. We are now more heavily populated than nature can provide for, and are forced to be industrious and assist nature to produce our increasing requirements. Our technologies, which have brought us better tools and weapons, have determined the direction of civilization's progress. In the presence of these evolutionary pressures none of us can isolate ourselves from the presence of others and revert back to subsisting solely on the provisions of nature, for there are no areas left devoid of civilization's congestion on which anyone could do so.

Our advancing technology has allowed us to more effectively aid nature in providing us with an abundance of food, and has given us the surpluses that allowed others to pursue trades which provide us with the implements and tools to continually increase our efficiency. This has given us the leisure and the means with which to attend to our pleasures and comforts. We no longer need continue to compete as nature encourages, and hope to leave our present political and national controversies behind us; creating the peace and plenty that our intellectual species is capable of achieving. I do not recommend that we attempt to rectify the injustices of the past, for we have all suffered from our previously unavoidable competitions. I only hope create the conditions that will prevent these barbaric activities from continuing onward into the future.

In the absence of politically created economic class levels we should no longer be critical of others economic successes, and would have less to gripe about. In being freed from the discriminations that raise or lower our economic status we would become equal with respect to the law and in our dealings with our administration. With population control we would no longer be in contention with our neighbors for sufficient resources to exploit, for the earth has plentiful areas on which limited numbers could find the means to live happily and contentedly upon. They would continue to improve their standard of living as they developed the techniques and took advantage of nature's consistencies and variations. While our species may never come to completely avoid nature's undesirable competitive influences, our recognition of them should allow us to intelligently respond to enhance our prospects despite their presence.

Our exploitation of the planet's area would likely be reduced, for we would wish to set aside areas for the preservation of nature's genetic variations. We would wish to keep these available for ongoing research in crossbreeding: developing disease-resistant plants, for concocting medications, as well as other miscellaneous purposes. We would be removed from the national pressure to continually increase production to remain in the forefront in the race for supremacy. Therefore, the areas that we set aside could be of a sufficient size. They would be sanctuaries for wildlife, not amusement parks for tourists, and must remain virtually unexploited to achieve our objectives. They should stay in their natural state because we would have enough areas remaining to provide for the needs of our reduced and regulated population. In the areas in which we inhabited: birds, animals, and their predators would probably become more numerous as human populations declined. This would bring about economic conditions similar to those that were enjoyed by immigrants to the Western Hemisphere, before it became overcrowded and polluted by the spread of our uncontrolled and ravenous civilization.

The pressures on our nonrenewable natural resources would be reduced and we could come into a desirable balance with all of our other resources. In turn, this would allow at first, one son or daughter, and generations later, two descendants to inherit the family farm or business, or the share-holding in a larger enterprise which provided their income. We would not be driven to migrate to less populated areas in search of greater opportunities and we would have sufficient resources to live happily and contentedly in the area that sustained us. We would still have acid rain and polluted waters, but on a reduced scale. Hopefully our freedom from excessive taxation and costly competitive activities will give us the affluence to devote more of our profits toward keeping our planet clean and livable.

We have calculated our planetary motions and have set our clocks accordingly. We have come to understand the realities of our environment and the forces that nature impose upon us. We have learned how to defy gravity: navigate upon water, and through air and space. We are a power second only to nature and have made many synthetic materials: even isotopes not previously found on earth. We, who have discovered the power of the atom, need only fear our inability to act wisely and constructively with the assets at our disposal. Likewise, by creating economic conditions not found in nature, we can overcome our need to compete. So let us use our common sense and refrain from exploiting each other, while the resources of the earth and the universe can fulfill our every need. There can be no greater inheritance. We can wish for nothing greater, for everything before us is ours. So I would like to ask, and then to answer, the all-important question that should be on everyone's mind.

May we act now, or must we wait to put our divided world and its mixed-up inhabitants on the right course, so that we can live noncombatively and contentedly?

We dare not wait for nature to take its course, so we must begin. We begin as I have begun, by sowing the seeds of change. When people become aware of the realities of our environment and have shed their antiquated superstitions, we can begin to put theory into practice.

We must unite the nations and be free of national conflict so we can lay down our weapons of mass destruction. Then we will have to halt the contentious division of the populace by politicians who try to appease one segment of the populace while alienating the other. Peace must be made at home, as well as abroad, for peace and contentment must begin in the heart of the individual. I will not dwell upon the intricacies of our transformation into a new world order, for it will depend upon how and when future majorities decide to do so. All we must do is to produce a workable plan; then the demand of the people will cause change to come naturally.

Without question, we are the rulers of our planetary domain, and are able to guide the course of civilization. We must not let the mistakes and misconceptions of the past destroy our future. We are unique, and are only limited by the length of our life span and the distances we can travel through space. The universe is ours to enjoy when we get there, and so shall be our utopia on earth when we learn to live at peace with each other.

5

Tend to your Marbles

(The trusting and the unwary are the easiest to fleece)

The previous chapter is basically an outline for a society that has embarked upon reducing its numbers to a level where the earth's resources could sustain them for generations to come. It will be added to and enlarged by many as we make the break from being ruled by nature to being ruled by intelligent foresight, causing this science to evolve as future generations gain the insight to guide their civilization on a desired course.

During the ensuing generations we hope to unite our societies, reduce our numbers, and overcome our natural instincts to take the fruits of others' labors. By providing sufficient opportunity for individuals to earn their needs through exploiting planetary resources, there should no need for people to exploit each other. We must make peace amongst ourselves and cooperate in making and abiding by laws which reduce and hopefully eliminate the predations upon the productivity of others. Thereby halting the redistribution of their earnings by conniving politicians attempting to please an overbearing and self-righteous majority. By first eliminating the need, and then the legality of doing so, we would be able to achieve peaceful coexistence and develop a morality supported by law. This should help close the gap between the many conflicting standards we presently live by. In this way, with our moral and legal standards in agreement we would be able to bring justice to the aggrieved, peace to the competitive and give protection to those that are being fleeced by those profiting from the loopholes and grey areas between morality and legality.

It is natural that our wisdom and abilities should grow as we learn more about ourselves and the world about us. Early man, not understanding the competitive influences of nature had no hope of settling differences with neighboring clans and was forced to rely upon physical might and advancing technology. Within his ethnic clan and society, early man relied upon the teachings of morality and the enforcement of spiritual and legal doctrines. This has given us much protection from the physical aggression of our neighbors and fellow countrymen, but it has done nothing to dampen the rivalry between nations.

In the modern business world, the abusive and injurious acts of the contestants cannot be completely eliminated, for there are always new ways to defraud people that our lawmakers have not foreseen. As well as the blue-collar crime of the employees, there is the white-collar crime of the owners and managers of private and public enterprises. The owners of private companies are in a position to scoop some of the profits of their enterprise, and so gain tax-free income by virtually stealing from themselves. The managers and directors of multiply-owned or public-traded companies are also in this same advantageous position and are able to defraud their shareholders or partners in many devious ways. These activities are usually conducted behind closed doors, or when no one is looking and since no violence is involved it is usually up to the injured party to seek redress in the civil courts.

Many companies are efficiently-operated and profitable and they grow in size according to the popularity and success of their products. However, the directors in many instances determine the speed and extent of growth and in most cases increase their salaries and perks according to the company's profitability.[3] Many take advantage of their insider position with a company to trade in shares before news is released to the public. Others use their administrative positions to profit through bid-rigging, paybacks, or by swinging sweet deals towards relatives and accomplices. The directors of many listed companies can and do defraud their shareholders by using all of the scams that they can devise, and when they are confronted with their crimes the stockholders are rarely compensated, for the booty has disappeared and the culprits have moved on to the next jurisdiction.

Newly registered companies appear on the stock market lists even faster than those that get delisted for not abiding by the exchange's requirements. An entrepreneur wishing to float a new public issue provides a prospectus and approaches a brokerage agent for financing. There is no set limit as there is in a bank loan, and the financer more often than not demands from sixty to seventy percent for risking their capital on the venture. This high rate reduces the percentage the new company receives for exploration or to develop and sell its product, and has led to the failure of many a venture.

After financing a project, the brokerage house promotes and

3. This is comparable to our representatives in government setting their own salaries and allowances at exorbitant levels, which goes to show you how little control the citizens or stockholders presently have over those that govern to suit themselves.

offers the initial issue of shares to the public. As well, the directors of a company prepare news-releases to promote interest in their venture so as to sell additional offerings of shares to raise money to operate the company toward profitability. Most new issues are popular with investors, for they gain in price while they are initially promoted. After the underwriters have unloaded their shares, and further share offerings have watered down the investor's equity, the perceived value and share price deteriorates if there is not a spectacular find or news of financial success.

At annual company meetings the directors that own large blocks of shares usually vote to give themselves options to purchase shares at a price approved by the stock market authorities. If the share price increases they can purchase shares at the option price, resell them the same day, and pocket the difference. Therefore, it is advantageous for both the directors and employees who may have been provided with incentive options to work toward making the company profitable. If this does not happen the next best thing is to make it appear that the company has found a store of treasure, and will soon be rolling in wealth.

There are two standard assay methods that closely indicate the amount of mineral in a drill-core. However some disreputable directors send their samples to assay offices that are out of the country, and that use methods that show greater values. Such news-releases boost the share price and the insiders of a company can sell their options at a greater profit. It seems that at times there is more money made financing and promoting the ventures than is spent in searching for the elusive resource.

I know of an instance where the directors of a company became the middle men in selling the company more mineral claims at an enormous personal profit to themselves, and in doing so depleted the company's treasury to the extent that it couldn't carry on with its earlier exploration commitments. In some instances directors will get into the business of providing a service to a company they control, and so are able to funnel a company's money into their own pocket by charging exorbitant rents or fees. As a result of such dealings, which are not at arms length, it is not surprising that so many companies go bankrupt. The shareholders are defrauded, and the directors walk off scot-free with their pockets full and in many instances promote other new ventures on the stock exchanges and do it all over again. As the result of the Securities Commissions inability to curtail the freedom that conniving directors have to arrange a company's dealings so as to enrich themselves, we would be wise not to invest in ventures over which we have no control. Instead, we should gain better control of the enterprises that we are or must be shareholders in.

We are competitors amongst other competitors, and it is not safe to invest in a business venture unless we have a say in the management of it. Mutual fund and pension fund managers usually buy a large block of shares in a thriving enterprise, and gain a seat on the board of directors. This protects their clients from insider scams and contributes to the profitability and popularity of such funds. This is a tactic that most successful managers resort to, and which allows some funds to greatly outperform others. The public's speculation on the stock markets usually does not provide them with an influence upon management and they frequently lose their money when the directors bilk them. The Securities Commission cannot look at every deal or effectively guard a shareholder's equity. Neither can our law enforcement agencies prevent us from being defrauded in private dealings. So we must conclude that managers of public companies are no more honest than the public at large, and are also tempted to profit by betraying the trust that is put in them. However, trust is something we have learned in Sunday school, and not in the business world. Those controlling larger treasures have more to gain, so I must say, "crime pays handsomely, white collar-crime pays most handsomely."

We are members of a competitive society and have developed considerable business know-how. To be successful we must learn how to protect our marbles from the other kids, our chickens from hungry coyotes, and our other valuables from those that conspire to take them from us. We should come to understand that larceny exists and be watchful for those that attempt to fleece us. We are clever enough to operate a business enterprise and to monitor the efficiency and honesty of our employees, so we should be able to oversee our governmental departments the same way. We all should be able to understand that it is not desirable for our governing body to interfere in a discriminatory manner in the economies of private enterprise. By not doing so we can halt the political controversies and reward the people that direct their energies exclusively toward producing their requirements from the limited available areas and resources of our planet.

With a central government we can eliminate war. With the regulation of population we increase our opportunities for prosperity. With the abolition of political discrimination we should have economic justice and peace of mind. Surely, those that are fully employed exploiting the resources of the planet, would have no reason to complain. Therefore, it is the unworthy and those that are determined to live off the efforts of others that we must protect ourselves from.

The enterprise in which we all will become shareholders would be that of setting up and operating our world government. We would only be concerned with operating one economic unit, making it desirable that we formulate legislation that would allow all of us the opportunity to earn our needs in an unmolested and honest manner. The rules that we agree to live and play by, should give us equal benefits or dividends as shareholders. We must demand that the administrators of this enterprise give us full and timely disclosure of all governmental activities, and account for all transactions, so that we can monitor their honesty. When our government buys something, we will wish to know how much it costs, and when they sell something, we will also wish to know how much was received. In this way, with the books open to all we would have the knowledge to run our governmental departments efficiently, for we should know by now that the opportunities are greater for those that stand by the cash register.

We presently rely upon others of greater experience or education to fix our gadgets or cure our illnesses, but our politicians gain their popularity by how well they please those that elect them. They do this by enacting legislation that appeases the majority by providing them with desired services and economic advantages. Consequently, we end up being led by the influence of the majority who demand expenditures on their behalf in excess of the governmental revenues generated. As well as being highly discriminatory, the resulting legislation is leading us all to the poorhouse–only our better judgement warns us that neither our obliging politicians nor their supporters can continue to raid the treasury without dire consequences. Our per capita debt is increasing and we are putting off the day when we must tighten our belts. So in essence, there is no leader except the will of the masses. No one to save us from our foolish spending spree except ourselves. We must manage our financial affairs more wisely and learn enough about economics to realize that you cannot spend next year's income, or go into debt without suffering the consequences.

We all may wish for an invincible leader, and like little children lost in the void we need a protective parent and a guiding hand. However, there is no universal protector to save us from our follies--our boastful representatives in government are mostly looking after their own skins--so it is we who must use our limited experience and knowledge to oversee the management of our planetary assets in which we will all be shareholders. It is we who must maintain the support and respect of all the shareholders by demanding that everyone be treated fairly and receive equal dividends.

We have learned how to increase the production of desirable commodities, and how to operate an efficient business enterprise so as to fulfill our needs and provide ourselves with financial security. We also must learn how best to oversee and run our governmental departments so that they become as efficient as those in the private sector. To do so effectively, we must have open access to the financial records to determine the efficiency of our governmental enterprises. I am of the opinion that television and computer networks can be utilized to a greater extent to teach us more about economics, as well as to keep us informed and able to guide ourselves on a just and noncombative course.

The use of electronic equipment would allow us to eliminate the thousands of teachers that teach the same subject-matter in our schools. With the enforcement of discipline before a TV screen we may even be able to eliminate the cost of building and transporting students to large learning centers. Children must learn to live and play together, but sometimes playgrounds are not supervised very well. Surveillance equipment probably could be used to a greater extent to identify bullies and counter the violent activities of cliques and gangs. By teaching our youngsters to respect each others' rights, we should hope to create an adult population with the morality to cease ganging up on its weaker factions. The wisdom and the power of majority must enforce the methods by which we can lead our civilization toward peace and plenty, but the majority should not continue to use their corruptive influence on government to enact and enforce laws which give them an economic advantage over their minorities. These competitive and immoral activities must come to a halt, for those that are deprived of economic equality will naturally resist, being motivated to separate nationally, or to use the weapons that our technology has developed to overcome the degradation that is imposed upon them. Peace within our schoolyards and outside of our schoolyards can only be made by discouraging the competitive activities and overcoming the need to compete amongst ourselves.

Getting back to the subject of our advancing technologies, automated devices save labor and allow industry to remain efficient and compete more successfully. We should not desire to protect the jobs and outdated trades of the past, but to encourage the advance of technology so that our daily productivity and our standard of living is enhanced.

It is not invincible leaders that we should look to, but an informed public that is capable of using its collective wisdom to surmount the obstacles in its path. This we do not learn in Sunday school or in church; so it would be best if we learned more about the actual conditions on our planet, and how to cope with them.

Our individual societies and nations are forced by natural conditions to compete and oppose each other in order to survive. We can prevent our wars, and the need for war by uniting them. The competition and pressure by individuals and groups to influence their government to provide economic advantages at the expense of others must be discouraged. We must have political peace along with national peace, then we can attend to the shortages we face that drive us to malign our neighbors. Our legislation should not be the method by which we compete for survival, for it is nature that we must use and manipulate to serve our needs. Our new government must remain uncorrupted and uncorruptible, for it must continue to protect the equal rights of the individual from those that attempt to debase them.

With adequate resources to exploit as the result of regulating our numbers, our government must protect our equal right to prosper. We may not be physically and mentally equal, but we should not have to compete for economic equality for our legislation should not give some an advantage over others. Our world government must treat all as equal, and please all in order to stay in power. It would not have any wisdom that is not available to the individual, so it is fitting that individuals govern their enterprises and protect their equal rights through government as best they can. To do so effectively, they must learn and teach each other the intricacies of directing and overseeing governmental departments and in managing the production and sale of their produce. We have much to learn about the perils inherent in economic exploitation, but there are no intelligences greater than our own and nobody to stand behind us when we fail. We will experiment, make our own blunders, and then hopefully perfect our ways as the result of the experiences we have gained.

6

The Demon within us

(At least that's what the spiritualists tell me)

We all have physical and sensual needs, which demand fulfillment. Hunger, drives us in search of food. Loneliness, leads
us in search of others of our own kind. These are normal and
natural motivations, and are even experienced by less intelligent species. We are not different temperamentally or possessed
of original sin as our theologians explain; we are possessed of
normal bodily requirements which cause us to compete for
nature's resources, and to resort to aggressive acts upon others
to gain our needs. Mankind is doomed to eternal struggle for
survival, not through Adam having eaten the apple, but by
nature. The influences that motivate us to do evil and injurious acts to others of our own kind, constitutes our so-called sin.
If we cannot overcome our need to aggress, we will continue
to compete until doomsday.

Our Christian teachings ask us to live modestly and share
with those in need. Hopefully, this would allow all to gain the
necessities of life so that there would be no need for crime and

violence. However, these teachings did not put us on the road to economic self-sufficiency and conditions deteriorated. The Bible tells us to populate the earth, but it doesn't say when to stop. Our competitive societies could not stop, for those that did or that were thinly populated, were overrun by those who needed more land to accommodate the needs of their increasing populations. Our societies condemn the aggressive and unjust acts of the individual, but as a group they continue to compete for the resources of neighboring states, and for political advantage over their minorities. This type of competition is instinctive and typical of our species which has not been able to overcome its fate of eternal struggle and strife. "Man is possessed of original sin," our theologians proclaim, and because of this we should meekly and obediently not appeal the sentence that some believed has been handed down from above.

This is typical Christian philosophy, which has remained unquestioned and unquestionable by believers, but which must be contradicted to make way for the truths that can solve our earthly problems. The only evidence that we have of the development of life and of mankind is that which fossil records provide, and our modern theory of evolution is based upon that evidence. We must discard all beliefs and theories that have no evidence to support them. Before the development of our modern sciences the ancients had declared that God made the world and the species upon the earth. However, we have since found evidence that shows a progression of life forms that branched out to become the forerunners of our many related species. In challenging our superstitious beliefs; modern scholars are not attempting to replace one unfounded hypothesis with another, but to portray the past according to the evidence at hand.

Of all the species: man became the most advanced in the

development of mental capabilities, and as a result became the most dominant. Our species is as perfect as nature has made us. It is not mankind, but nature, which is imperfect. It allows species to increase in numbers to the extent that they are forced to compete for the territory and resources that sustains them. It allowed man's groupings to evolve in size; increasing their competitive might, to become the highly organized and powerful nations of our day. We must overcome our inability to provide ourselves with material sufficiencies by controlling our numbers so that we can live above the competitive level, for nature drives us to compete as it does other beasts.

We have learned how many cows to put in a pasture in order to have contented animals, but have not been able to use the same remedy to improve our lot, for we are locked into a competitive struggle where the power of numbers has been an advantage. There has been no one to lead us in the past but we have now become wise enough to avoid the undesirable consequences of our competitive activities, and should design our government so that it serves and supports our intellectual objectives. However, the public's demands to fulfill its physical requirements will continue to guide us, for that is the singular objective of life. The drive to satisfy the demands of our senses is not the disease that blights us. It is the magnet that leads us toward the fulfillment of them. Let not ignorance and superstition stand in our way, for nature is our servant, not our master.

In the Heart of Welfare City
(and their wish list is plain to see)

7

Some Rhyme and Reason

(So let's be reasonable)

In this modern era we are able to visualize ancient times and understand the part played by nature in causing species to instinctively compete for survival. Mankind became the most intelligent and capable and was able to outperform all others. We compete against other species, and also amongst ourselves for the resources of the earth. However, we must become more than the greatest competitor of all time. We must overcome the need to compete amongst ourselves in order to achieve peaceful coexistence. Our exploitation of the resources of the planet and of each other is natural and instinctive, for nature rewarded the most successful. This continued to support the evolution of larger social groups or nations that outperformed and defeated smaller and less technically advanced groups. It is these aggressive activities, and the motives that cause them that we must do our best to eliminate. We must use our acquired knowledge to overcome our problems rather than let the competitive influences of nature determine our destiny.

The earth has sustained us in the past, and can continue to do so within its limitations in the future. Its resources are great, and we exploit them as a shepherd does his sheep and sheepdog, for we are the most intelligent and are in a position to take advantage of all other species. Human exploitation has become more concerted as our societies have grown in size; making our societies and national units a power that only similarly unified groups can successfully contend with. These competing nations are now the independent powers that must be united in order to bring peace and prosperity to humanity. Despite those that desire to protect their lucrative ruling positions, we must teach our societies the true nature of reality, so that they can prevent our civilization from following its predestined course.

Life's necessities, and our instinctive drive to gain them brings us into competition with our fellow man, for there is not enough opportunity for all. However, we need not let nature motivate our actions and rule us for we are now sufficiently intelligent and capable of uniting the rival nations, and regulating our numbers so as to get out of the grip of nature's rule. With increased resources and opportunities to produce our needs and with the cessation of the political redistribution of our profits, we will be able to leave the contentiousness of our competitive lifestyle for a peaceful one of our own design.

Civilizations throughout history have risen and fallen, with the survivors starting anew. While societies have wished to avoid repeating the obvious mistakes of the past, there have been no alternatives available to them. They have had to continue the competitive lifestyle of their predecessors, and improve upon the weapons and the techniques to dispense with their rivals more punctually and efficiently. Our national histories are riddled with accounts of economically inspired national aggressions, and it is a fact that mankind has been unable to find lasting peace and plenty upon this planet. At this late date in time we can better predict the future course of civilization by knowing the course that it has followed in the past. It does appear that necessity is driving us to compete and progress toward greater technical ability, and our ignorance of reality has prevented us from making the needed changes that would alter the course of civilization.

The principal conflicts of recent decades have been between large capitalist and socialist blocs of nations. The race is on, and the most advanced and productive will supersede the other. Our leaders are determined to win the race between the hare and the tortoise, or Capitalism and Socialism if you like, for they are as competitive as the rest of us and strive to be the winners. It has been more important to preserve ourselves and our system of government, than to preserve the ecology of our planet. Thus we have allowed pollution to go unchecked while we spent our energy in manufacturing weapons of war to maintain our dominant position, and our chances for survival. However, there can be no winners through continued competitiveness, for it surely will lead to our extinction by destroying our environment with our pollutants or through atomic warfare. We have no choice but to face the realities of our situation, otherwise we will continue to suffer the consequences of our failure to do so.

Our progress in the past has allowed us to resist the intrusions of other aggressive nations, but we now see clearly that the trend of our civilization's progress is toward self-annihilation. There is nothing wrong with progress when it is toward a desirable goal, but progress in our technical ability to destroy each other should be of greater concern to our societies—only they have the power to guide our civilization toward desired objectives.

Modern nations grew in size as they developed the transportation and communication facilities to govern larger areas. These advances allowed societies to trade and fight with each other and to explore and claim the undefended territories they found. The British, leading in the development of seagoing transportation, became the most noteworthy of those that overran and colonized the lands of the less advanced societies of the earth. At the height of their power, the British controlled a scattered empire that comprised approximately one-quarter of the land mass of the earth. Their objectives were economic, and they were motivated to exploit these territories for their crown and country. The stone-age inhabitants of these areas were not capable of stopping the advance of civilization and were pushed aside as the invaders settled on their hunting grounds and decimated the wild game that had sustained them. The immigrants exploited the newly acquired territory and the ruling nations exploited their colonies. In time the settlers began to realize that much of the profits of their labors were being sent back to the homeland, so they demanded to be released from their colonial status. Most have now been reluctantly given the freedom to govern themselves and become independent nations.

If the British had provided equal status to the citizens of their colonies, and not exploited them economically, they probably would have been able to hold their empire together and may have succeeded in extending it to unite all of the societies of the earth. However, the objective of the British, as well as other national groups was monetary gain, rather than world unification. Eventually, the oppressed were motivated to free themselves from the clutches of their oppressors. It is necessary for humans to respect each other's equality, and for our government to enforce laws that honor these rights, in order to persuade societies to give up the national security that they now have. Therefore, we must learn to respect the rights of all of our citizens. The benefits of peaceful coexistence can reward us all by eliminating the waste of political and national rivalry.

We can now see that it is necessary to bring the nations of the earth together in order to halt national conflict. We can also understand that we will have to abide by nonexploitative legislation to provide equality to all races and minority groups; thereby, creating the advantages and the desire to unite and to remain united. To overcome nature's detrimental influences, we must take control and create conditions so that we can reside in a peaceful and noncompetitive environment. While it will be necessary to become and to remain a member of a society that earns its requirements we must replace nature's competitive values, with values that would allow us to overcome our controversies. We have come to understand that no amount of physical fitness or technical might can save us from our competitive demise. To become able to do so humans must promote the truths of reality so that we can reap the benefits. We must teach the knowledge that has been discovered by our advancing sciences, so that we can intelligently guide our civilization which our forefathers in previous generations were incapable of doing.

We are truly a species shaped by the forces of nature, but we must not let it cause us to continue to compete for survival when we can make it serve our every need. Let mind triumph over matter, and let the intelligence of man bring us into the desired balance with our exploitable environment. The future of mankind is in our hands and the universe awaits us. What more

could we ask for when we have the ability to adjust our numbers according to the resources we require to live in harmony
upon it?

8

The Modern Day Robbing Hoods Must Depart

(And a few things the Little Johns should know)

Here's to the species of which it is advantageous to be a member of. Second only to the power of nature, but wise enough to escape its absolute control. Allowing us to guide the course of civilization so as to avoid riots and wars over economic matters through uniting our nations and regulating our numbers. However, nature can bring calamities upon us which we are not responsible for, and do not in any way contribute to. We can do nothing to prevent the devastation caused by changing weather patterns, shifting continental plates, or wandering comets. Extremes of weather are common and can destroy the produce of a season or more. Whether it be hail, drought, or flood, we must prepare for such eventualities by putting aside the profits of bountiful years. We can have our private insurance schemes or community assistance programs, but our government cannot get involved except to keep them honest. We would do our best to overcome misfortunes that can be brought about by destructive beasts and insects, and the disorders caused by germs and viruses. We would also be plagued with mutations, and other physical and mental defects in our offspring that would affect their ability to provide adequately for their needs,

Family members in our modern society share their food, and somewhat proportionately the living standard of their group. In times of prosperity, a family's necessities are plentiful. At other times, due to the variable nature of our business and weather cycles, income is reduced and only the necessities can barely be afforded. In the event of accident, illness, and age, or being abandoned by their chief provider, a family's living standard may deteriorate because of lowered production and income. In the recent past families supported their elders and invalids according to their ability and humanitarian instincts to do so. They were not able to cope with or support unlimited numbers of nonproducing relatives.

In living as nature provides, the strong, the quick, and the clever are able to garner their basic needs while the aged, ailing, and foolish fall prey to predators or otherwise fail to provide themselves with the necessities of life. It has been determined that cosmic rays can alter our genetic blueprint, and it is believed to be the major cause for the mutations that have brought forth new types and varieties of species. Some of these mutations provide individuals with advantages, but in most instances this is not the case, and the mutants die out for nature only supplies the opportunity for life according to the nutrients it supplies.

We are limited in the amount of aid that we could give to the ailing members of our family, and would be forced to be selective and abandon the most hopeless cases so as to provide for our own well-being. It is not that we would be lacking in humanitarian concerns, it is only that we are lacking in productive capacity and can only give away limited amounts. We are concerned about our sexual partners, our children, our parents, our brothers and sisters; but are less concerned about other families and their undisciplined kids. Our concern becomes less as their distance from us becomes greater, much like the air which gets thinner as distance from the earth increases. We are willing to work harder to aid someone near to our heart, but would not put out the same effort for someone we do not know.

To provide social assistance programs, or a safety net for the needy and the ailing, has been a popular platform for our political parties. These practices have become entrenched and continued by following administrations, for they play on our sympathies for the plight of others, and relieve us of the responsibility to aid family members when they become incapacitated or face emergencies. Consequently, the government has taken it upon itself to support growing numbers of mutants that are plagued by a variety of genetic disorders and malfunctions, those that are incapacitated as the result of injury, disease, or substance abuse, those awaiting unemployment insurance cheques, and those whose unemployment insurance has expired, landed immigrants and refugees that are awaiting immigration hearings, and are not allowed to accept employment while they wait.[4] Additionally, we have our own home-bred and educated welfare bums that find it more expedient to become a recipient than a contributor. In the Canadian northland and on Indian reservations virtually entire communities receive

---

4. It has been a practice for the Immigration Department in Canada to provide for new arrivals until they have their hearings. This acquaints them to an easy way of life that they are reluctant to leave, but there is much pressure upon our politicians to allow new immigrants to earn their keep rather than become a liability to the nation. Recently the government has set a fee so as to recover these early costs. Hopefully, this will lessen the drain on the treasury and provide us with some worthy citizens whose work ethic has not been corrupted. However, the regulations are continually changing so this ruling may have been repealed.

social assistance in one form or another, and we find ourselves supporting increasing numbers of idle people from the public purse, that we could not and would not support from our own pockets. However, our government will not be able to do so much longer; it has got itself into debt, and is running out of producers that can withstand the higher taxation rates that are needed to support the increasing costs of our politically sponsored social assistance programs.

When we personally become bankrupt; we find ourselves with insufficient funds to meet our obligations, and no one willing to give us more credit to operate our mortgaged enterprise. Our governments are in a more advantageous position, they do not allow the economy of our society to collapse, and so do not declare bankruptcy. The politicians protect their jobs and the economy of the nation by printing more money, or by otherwise devaluing the currency, and allowing inflation to halve their debts. In the presence of inflation, lenders must be offered higher interest rates to encourage the purchase of bonds. As the government becomes more deeply indebted, the cost of servicing their debt becomes greater; leaving less revenue to provide for the desired public services. Consequently, we find that our government is no more able to continue to fund nonproducers than we are individually; in both cases the number of nonproducers that can be supported is dependent upon our productive abilities and surpluses.

Hopefully, we all are able to calculate and understand that the proceeds from the sale, or rental of our resources, and from taxation, will not be sufficient for our government to support growing numbers of social assistance claimants. The percentage of claimants goes up as the percentage of producers falls, giving our government a declining tax base as its costs spiral.

Therefore, we or our government must choose amongst the applicants and direct our efforts to aid those that are most important to us, or are mendable and have a greater potential to become self-supporting again. The survival of a healthy society is dependent upon its members being able to produce their needs. It makes more sense to save our industrious society, so as to maintain our standard of living, than attempt to save the growing numbers of nonproducers who are beyond our ability to provide for. We do not wish to take away anyone's right to life, liberty, or happiness, but these rights are directly connected to our ability to provide for ourselves. Thus in actuality, we earn these rights through producing our needs. We are not in an economic position to provide the necessities of life to large numbers that do not earn them, so we must let nature and human nature determine who shall survive to reproduce more of their own kind.

We will wish to maintain and better our living standards. We must support the values of a productive society, and prevent its producers from being financially throttled by our government's practice of supporting increasing numbers of deviants who demand the benefits of toil, without supplying a fair share of the energy. We are a working society, and a very fair society that does not wish to deny anyone the right to vote. However, we must outlaw political discrimination; and in taking the political bribes off the shelf, there will be much to be gained and nothing left to vote for.

We all require food and desire the security and conveniences that wealth can provide. Some of us are willing to work harder, or put in longer hours to upgrade our living standards, or to save for a rainy day. In most cases we are deserving; having earned what we provide for ourselves. The well-off do not owe anything to those that are inefficient and unproductive, except their sympathy.

Our politicians find it advantageous to hand out lucrative government contracts and loans to labor intensive industries that donate large sums to their treasuries. These practices give a favored company an advantage, and to be able to pay their employees above average wages. Sometimes the government is swayed by powerful labor groups to give out contracts that stipulate that the work must be performed by unionized employees. This assures the presiding politicians that the union membership will support them in the next election. Sometimes labor unions hold the producers of commodities at ransom by conspiring with other organized labor groups, and block exports at the terminals if the commodities are not handled by unionized dock-workers and loaded onto unionized ships. With political parties in collusion with organized labor they are able to feather each other's nest.

In Canada there are large areas that are suitable for the production of grain. A large portion of the grains grown are surplus to domestic requirements, and are exported to other nations. Grain growers have not been able to limit their production to achieve higher domestic prices and have to rely on foreign markets. In selling their grains overseas Canadian producers must compete with producers in other countries where the standard of living and wages are very low. As a consequence, profits are dependent upon the yield of their crops and the prices on the world market minus the cost of rail transport and the demands of labor unions at the export terminals. Most grain producers use their own elevators throughout the prairies, which own the terminals which load the ships. Farmers also have formed a union but they have been unable to oust the powerful labor unions that became entrenched in their export marketing facilities. However, our vote buying politicians will not act in opposition to the labor unions that support them and as a consequence, farmers get no help from government or from the police in overcoming the stranglehold that the unions have at the terminals and on the high seas. The general public also do not get any help when they try reducing our politician's salaries, pensions and perks; for we have given them the power to manipulate the economy to advantage themselves.

Political control of our economy creates an artificial multi-classed society, and those that work the hardest or are the most efficient do not always receive the financial rewards that are due to them. When politicians conspire with labor unions to safeguard their positions, we should have reason to complain and revolt for we do not wish to appease those that debase our earnings to increase their own. In order to treat us equally, government cannot discriminate amongst us and give cause for its overthrow. Natural circumstances create economic class levels that are more justifiable. The weather plays a large part in determining costs and quantities of production in agriculture. Fluctuating prices at the marketplace can determine our prosperity in both agriculture and manufacturing. Our health and our ability to produce also play a large part, so we will have those who are poor or unable to provide for themselves among us on a permanent basis.

To hunt for, or to gather nature's provisions as we did in the past, to grow crops, or to manufacture the needs and wants of our civilization, are not always the most enjoyable ways to spend one's time. However, in our advanced civilization it is necessary that we work to supply our increasing requirements, for nature can only support low population densities. To work for an employer, or to be self-employed does not always provide the income we desire, so there has been much planning and experimentation to develop easier and more profitable ways to earn a living. The development of mechanization during the Industrial Revolution gave us greater productive capacity, and allowed us to increase our income and upgrade our living standards. We are now in an age in which electronics and automated devices ease our labors, and increase our productivity still more.

This prosperity has given our governments the ability to raise fees and taxes to help achieve national objectives; as well as to provide subsidies to make the nation self-sufficient in its requirements, and to provide exports to balance the nation's imports. It has also given our political parties larger revenues with which to subsidize their supporters, and to give lucrative appointments to friends and party members, as well as to raise their own salaries, pensions, and perks to exorbitant levels. These discriminatory practices have divided the citizens into various political factions, each squabbling for a share of the favors, and resulting in periodic elections (in the free world) to decide which group will reward their constituents and supporters.

Our politicians need the support of the voters to stay in power and there is no better way to do this than to buy the public's support with the monies that have been taken from them. Most forms of discrimination have been outlawed, but political discrimination divides us into opposing groups. We do not need political or any other form of discrimination in our midst and should not allow it to continue. Those that promote our present survival values, or artificially manipulate the profits of productivity, will be able to take a few breaths while they decide what to do with themselves. We should not wish to have our public funds continued to be used in a manner that discriminates, and causes dissension among us. We should wish to be able to live in peace and respect with others that do not take our earnings to give themselves a better house, or longer holidays than we have for ourselves. The factors of supply and demand at our public marketplaces can set the value of commodities that are for sale, and compensate us more fairly for our work--at no cost to us.

Weather and market fluctuations will affect our prosperity, but we must accept the fortunes and misfortunes that circumstances bring to our door. Those that are not industrious or do not produce anything tangible should not be supported with public funds. In our populous society we survive and prosper through our ability to earn our needs through exploiting the resources of the planet. As an intelligent species, we should not allow ourselves to continue to be exploited by others. With the uniting of the nations, the subsidization of nonproducers and the promotion of ecological destroying masses will no longer be necessary. We would no longer need the cannon fodder. Neither would it be wise to support nonproducers to the extent that their numbers could outvote or enslave the worthy producers of our society.

We are a cunning as well as a resourceful creature, and if we can enhance our financial position without great risk or effort we are inclined to do so. As our representatives in government climb up the administrative ladder they take charge of ever greater amounts of capital and their opportunities to divert larger amount from the treasury become greater. We can demand an accounting from our lower ranking civil servants, but we are unable in many instances to gain truthful answers or an accounting from the party in power. They make the rules and have a controlling influence over the judges in our courts. Political parties do not voluntarily run their own departments honestly or eliminate their own extravagance and corruption. Neither do our police forces satisfactorily discipline themselves, for in many instances further investigation reveals irregularities and coverups.

Birds of a feather are inclined to band together, so our governmental departments are inclined to shield and provide alibis for each other to maintain their integrity as a group. We should not be surprised to find that our government and its employees are no more honest than the rest of us. We are all motivated to achieve our financial objectives, and when we gain them most of us set a higher goal as there is no limit to the extravagance that wealth can provide. One could presume that we are all looking for easy ways to get rich, but some go about accumulating their wealth more honestly than others.

The inability of our governments to restrain the abuse of their social assistance programs has made our treasuries the target of many scams. In taking over our obligation to fend for ourselves our governments have been unable to limit the increasing numbers that have found it easy to garner a monthly assistance cheque and to qualify for free dental and medical coverage. This has opened the door to other profitable opportunities, for then many in going from doctor to doctor run up huge costs in getting physicians to prescribe the free pain killers, which they then sell on the street. Others use our government's unmanageable open-arms policies to fund a lifetime of leisure, or to even raise a family at taxpayers' expense. Thereby, fostering second and third generations that habitually and skillfully remain on the dole. Only those that are closely associated with those that are failing to provide adequately for themselves would know whether they are faking, and only they could regulate the giv-

ing of charity according to need. However, they would probably be inclined to be more generous if they were using someone else's money rather than their own.

While we are sympathetic to those that have come into dire
straights as the result of marital breakdown, injury, disease, or
death, most hard working citizens are not willing to be ripped
off continuously by growing numbers that are just as capable
of providing for themselves as they are. It is not right that the
most industrious and productive be brought to their knees
through taxation, to support those that are unwilling and unable
to contend with the shortage of opportunity our civilization has
come to experience. This shortage has naturally occurred as a
result of too many people vying for the exploitable opportunities that are available, and some succeed while others fail.

In Europe, it became a custom among the landholders for
the eldest son to inherit the family hectares. They could not
continue to divide it amongst the children, for then there would
not be enough for any one of them to earn a living on the
reduced areas. Immigration to the colonies provided the needed
opportunities and the world's population continued to double
and redouble.

In most areas of the earth our species face the same lack of
opportunity. Many take jobs and work for others. Some are
ambitious enough to save so that they can start a business of
their own. A growing number do not expend sufficient energy
so as to give an employer an honest day's work. They become
chronically unemployed and many only desire to work long
enough to qualify for unemployment insurance again. When
employers no longer wish to rehire the light-fingered and lazy,
they remain unemployed and unemployable. Finding themselves in this position, many apply for governmental assistance

for educational upgrading or while supposedly looking for a job which they likely would not hold for long, even if they were successful in finding one.

With the comfortable lifestyle that our Social Assistance programs have provided, an unwed mother need only fill out the forms for assistance. Then she is free to party with those that can afford to show her a good time. The children learn to ignore the indignity of having the taxpayers be their provider, and learn the scams by which they can increase and prolong the take.

There is a lack of opportunity and there is nothing we can do except overcome this shortage. The government cannot determine who is rightfully deserving, or afford to finance them even if they are truly in despair. The cost of raising and educating children must be born by the parents, and those that wish to participate in the bounties of our civilization's production will again have to earn the price.

With the amalgamation of the nations, we would no longer need to remain numerically competitive. The industrious would no longer be forced to support unneeded and unwanted population densities. Those participating in our civilization's attempts to increase the earth's productivity would find greater opportunities to earn their needs as the population declined and reached a desired balance with our available resources. Our environmentally wrecking population explosions and exploitations would have come to an end. Our planet's great potential would be developed through avoiding the competitive influences of nature, thereby, bringing the opportunity for peace and prosperity to a species that earns and deserves the contentment it provides for itself.

Giving people a welfare cheque is much like feeding the pigeons in the park. At first there are only a few, but later as they find it easier than looking for food elsewhere. More flock in, followed by their young who find out where the goodies are. So like the pigeons: our welfare roles grow larger and larger, while the conspiracies to get on or stay on the roles become more numerous. Normal employment on which income-tax and unemployment insurance is deducted by an employer may reduce or disallow a recipient's eligibility to claim welfare, so many recipients in avoiding such income look for and earn income that they can hide from the government. Recipients of welfare or unemployment insurance frequently conspire with an employer to work at a reduced wage and receive their pay on the sly. Others become involved with alcohol or drugs to while away their spare time. Females frequently take to prostitution to support a drug habit while still remaining on the welfare roles. Males more often take to pimping, drug dealing, and other predatory activities.

Theft, deceit, and violence become a way of life to many that are ripping off the system, and are looking for other easy ways to profit while they wait for the next welfare cheque. One could say that the welfare system rewards and encourages fraud, corrupts people, and makes them criminals. Having been convicted of a crime and serving time in jail it is common practice for inmates to brazenly continue to con the system by leaving their identification cards with an accomplice on the outside who then fills out the necessary forms, and picks up and cashes the assistance cheques while the other is incarcerated.

Many American Indians and Eskimos are particularly reluctant to accept the productive ways of the white man and produce their needs by modern methods. They tell their children that since the invaders have taken their hunting grounds without compensation, they should now make the honkies look after them. Some have even been known to loan their children to each other, so that they can fool the welfare workers and gain increased allowances. People that are able to gain regular assistance cheques from the government do not find it as necessary to work full-time as others do. They are able to avoid being employed, to the same extent that they become subsidized. Some are even able to scrape by from month to month without working at all, while others can only manage to spend their Christmases and the cold winter months in jail. Anyway, this unearned income buys a lot of free time (for those that are fed and sheltered by the government) to party and get into mischief. This keeps the police and paramedics busy looking after those that have been victimized, or have passed out in public places. The working class wonder where it will all lead to. Our befuddled politicians are at a loss as to how to put a stop to it without losing votes and revenue from liquor sales, while the clamor on skid row is for the development of more low-rental housing so as to make room for more of them. However, the developers know who are the most reliable tenants and the taxpayers wonder when it will be their turn to get something for nothing. But it can never be for they have been conditioned to work and earn, and are the gift-horse. While the parasites, like flees on a dog, complain about legislated poverty and encourage our politicians to tax the industrious and propertied at a higher rate.

The fact that our elected government can be manipulated by pressure groups and majorities to provide tax-exemptions and subsidies, makes our government the target of every con artist in the land. The world does not owe anyone a living, three meals a day, or an easy job that pays high wages. Nature does not supply these so we must strive to earn our needs and to better conditions for the human race by using our physical and mental abilities. During this century's industrial revolution we increased our productivity tremendously, giving us the ability to gain greater economic security and to reduce our working hours or years, thereby upgrading our living standard. However, this did not give us the ability to survive without working. We would do well to share the work again, so that we can better the quality of life and gain the economic security we strive for.

While our early close-knit family groups have evolved into larger states and nations, the feeling of family has been lost, and the citizens have ceased to voluntarily share the profits or the labor which brings it into existence. Individuals have become more financially independent of each other but our politicians in promoting the might of numbers, have legalized methods to redistribute the profits of the industrious to support those that are unable or unwilling to earn their keep. With competition for governmental handouts, we have ended up with a society that is beset with contention and controversy in the scrambles to get at the freebies. Humans are devious creatures and wishing the ease and the security that a redistribution of the fruits of labor brings about, have found ways to become permanent recipients of our Social Assistance programs. Our financially sharing political parties gain popularity by doing this and the recipients holler for more. Many are determined to continue to live off the profits and productivity of others while those that work and earn have become a slave to the state. We must free the industrious from excessive taxation, and stop the handouts in order to encourage the population to share the work, and regain the prosperity that a fully-employed society is capable of achieving.

As things stand, almost everyone from millionaires down to beggars on the street consider the government and the public purse to be the goose and the golden eggs. We now have allowed our government to become deeply in debt and must discontinue expensive subsidies and unmanageable social programs in order to balance the books. In the absence of national rivals we will no longer need to protect our borders, and must discontinue political and social practices that have taken advantage of the industrious. Individuals must be freed from political oppression, and allowed to expend their surplus energy to attend to their own personal priorities and desires. After an adequate tax to finance our public services, there should be no social pressure to force industrious people to spend their earnings in a manner that does not please them.

We have been taught much about the sanctity of life, but this belief is not supported by nature or even human nature. What nature provides is free for the taking, and we like dumb animals, have not overcome the necessity to compete for survival. We are mostly concerned with our family and personal needs, and normally do not have a great incentive to donate to strangers. Therefore, we must let those with the most concern for the unproductive supply the assistance that they are willing and able to give.

In the utopian eras of the future, where we will have eliminated national controversies and implemented population control, we would be able to reduce our working hours still further if we refrain from publically subsidizing the increase of the unproductive. It is those that can and do earn their subsistence and not the failures, that we should be more concerned about. Only they have the physical ability and the will to support themselves, and become a member of a group that is able to progress toward the peace and plenty that it requires. Like an automobile engine that is misfiring on one cylinder, we must prevent the one unproductive member of our society from becoming two and the two becoming four. In this way we will prevent the wheels of production from coming to a halt and our standard of living deteriorating rather than advancing toward the utopia we desire.

With sufficient opportunity, most healthy adults could earn more than their basic needs. They would gain the surpluses which would allow them to contribute to the charitable causes of their choice."Blood is thicker than water," they say, so what could be a greater cause than to aid an invalid offspring or relative in need. However, it is not desirous to let vote buying politicians and a recipient society determine how much we should pay, for charity begins in the hearts of donors and extends according to their wealth and concerns.

Death and higher taxes are all that our competitive nations and discriminating administrations can offer us. Believers in political wizardry demand more and higher costing social programs to ease their burdens and protect them from need, and the politicians must bow to this pressure to stay in power. If this trend continues, soon there will not be enough production to supply the goods, or producers who can outvote the consumers. When our government raises income and payroll deductions, or attempts to reduce their commitments in providing unemployment insurance, medical or pension coverage there is an outcry from those that have been paying the shot; as well as from those that pay the least, and want these programs continued or even increased. The same applies to welfare where we cannot keep the number of recipients and the costs in check. A government that would be long lasting could not continue to sponsor such schemes--where those that pay the most receive the least in benefits. We would have to discontinue these and all other vote-buying enticements that cause discrimination, for our future government must be supported by both the minorities and the majorities. We cannot have peace by trampling upon the minorities equal rights, for a revolutionary leader always comes from within the ranks of the oppressed.

Our leaders and representatives in government have become the modern day Robin Hoods. Taking from the rich and those with the incentive to earn, and giving to the unable and the unwilling. The tainted fruits of political handouts are much like the proceeds of crime; once experienced they become addictive, and ones need to work grows less. However, the ones that create such an ignominy cannot be prosecuted for their actions, for they pass laws to legalize their practice of taking and then giving to those that have not earned it. All those that are inclined to object too strenuously to such purse-lightening schemes gets an arrow straight to the heart.

Our society has become accustomed to wide-ranging social programs which contribute to governmental deficits. When we borrow personally we are restricted by our bankers to the amounts that we can safely pay back, but the public is the lender to the government when we buy their bonds. Our economic sense is not on a par with our bankers, and we are taken in by our politicians who offer to appease our desire for greater subsidies and services. We cannot afford to pay for such extravagance, and as a result our government is going further and further into debt. We and our representatives must quit raiding the treasury, but none are willing to be first to tighten their belt. We all desire the comforts and security that wealth can provide, but we must come to realize that in an ongoing society it is morally proper and considerate of future generations to not pass on our debts to them.

Many of us have come to believe that the redistribution of the wealth and earnings of the producers will make for a better tomorrow, but it is only better for those that are favored. The work load is shifted from one to the other. Some are driven to be more efficient and productive, while others can take it easy. Our production as a whole is not increased, and a higher standard of living does not materialize. Our politicians can juggle the coins and pass them out liberally, but they can only spend in excess of their revenues as long as they borrow and keep adding to the public debt.

This makes it necessary for our government to use larger portions of its revenue to pay interest, leaving dwindling amounts for the services we require and desire. Deficit spending can only lead to continued inflation which reduces the value of our savings and monetary security. We must come to understand the situation we are in, and refuse to be led down the garden path by deceptive and self-serving politicians. As an alternative, we must set up an administration that we can control, and which respects our right to limit production, set prices, and govern our economic affairs to our exclusive advantage. In doing so we must let nature and human nature determine the physical and mental attributes that must be maintained in order to produce our individual requirements, and to bring us the peace and plenty that this planet has to offer.

We must put a halt to all patronage and political subsidation of favored groups in order to prevent the deterioration of our society's work ethic. The incentive to look after invalids would be by those that are related or closely associated with them. They would be in a position to know the degree to which assistance was required, and would be able to recognize pretenders. They would also be limited in the number of mentally and physically incapacitated that they could afford to support. This would assure that our species prospered through its ability to produce in abundance, rather than degenerate because of the numbers that were unwilling or unable to provide for themselves. By freeing the taxpayers from the expense, and our government from the unwise and unmanageable task of determining the eligibility of nonproducers, we would be able to defeat the present scams perpetrated by welfare recipients crossing jurisdictional boundaries, or by having two or more identifications to process multiple claims. Virtuous adults would have second thoughts about bringing a child into the world where it would impose a hardship upon their acquaintances. And finally, there should be no desire on our part to allow domineering politicians to determine our charitable obligations, or to continue to waste public funds to hire unneeded social workers who may use their position to rip off the accursed system some more.

Yes, charity truly begins in the heart of the donor--but it also should end there. The course of civilization must be guided by our head rather than by our sympathy for others or by our instincts to fill our stomachs. We must set higher goals than simply using our powers to appropriate and redistribute the assets of others politically or militarily. We must use our heads to determine how best to deal with the powers of nature which have a controlling influence upon the prosperity of all the species that live on this planet.

In their terms in office, politicians attempt to please the majorities by redistributing the wealth that the workers of the nation have produced. They are the leaders of the most powerful gang within our society, and determine how best to advantage its members by depriving the minorities of economic equality. They do not create anything material by their own efforts, so cannot be our provider or the answer to our prayers. We need not look for miracles from that quarter. However, we need no gods to aid us in order to produce sufficient for our needs on this planet, nor should we be hindered by the devils of yesteryear. We have only nature and human nature to contend with.

We live in a real world so must face reality. Our earthly utopia can only be created by those with the bodily ability to bring it about. As intelligent human beings, we are able to determine the direction to take, and in doing so could guide the course of civilization. Our understanding of the environment should enable us to achieve the greatest prosperity our planet has to offer. So let us continue to advance our sciences and increase our abilities for as long as the sun continues to shine down upon us.

As I have written before, we are the only guiding power. The health of our society and the prosperity of our species is in our hands. Let us not deviate from the path that leads to our salvation.

According to the Merriam Webster Dictionary, Robin Hood was a legendary English outlaw who gave to the poor what he stole from the rich. This would seem to be morally justifiable for it provides the members of a society with a more equitable living standard.

Our representatives in government attempt to please their constituents by mocking this age-old practice of redistributing income. While they take from those that have earned, and give some to the needy, most use their administrative position to get as rich as circumstances provide. Taking bread from most tables to put caviar on their own. This is a long way from creating a just society, for on our overpopulated planet our needs are no longer supplied by nature. It is earned, so it is fitting that if we are to share the wealth with each other, then we also should share the toil that creates it.

To the Heights of Human Achievement
(And toward peace and plenty for our species)

9

A Review of Sorts

*(Once again for those I may have lost along the way,
and another chance for the author to belittle the Devil)*

We are the new generation and have come into possession of
the earth. It is all ours; the assets, the liabilities, and the knowledge. We have inherited the competitive lifestyle that natural
conditions encourage, and must defend what is ours and strive
for what is others in order to provide for the needs of our increasing numbers.

The natural course is for a species to compete for the necessities of life to the best of their physical and instinctive ability,
but for mankind (the most capable species on earth) the use and
manufacture of tools to enhance efficiency has provided advantages which have allowed the most advanced societies to outperform and overrun the territories of the poorly equipped. A
better tool or weapon increases our efficiency and power, and
as we improved upon their designs and increased their supply
we have become amazingly efficient and all-powerful. There
is nothing that can defeat us except natural calamities or oth-

ers of our own species. We must get away from the competitive lifestyle that natural conditions encourage and make peace with our neighbors.

Nature has allowed the species to compete numerically as well as technically. This has resulted in increased pollution of our environment from human and industrial wastes, and the likelihood of additional disruption of the ecology from the use of the more hazardous atomic fuels and weapons. As intelligent human beings, we should put a stop to activities that are dangerous to our health and well-being, for there can be more to life than the struggle and strife of our competitive existence.

The earth can be a suitable habitat for us for millions of years to come, but we must realize that it is limited in the life-sustaining resources that it can provide and govern ourselves accordingly. Nature's supplies have limited our numbers in the past, but with the use of agricultural methods we have increased the production of foodstuffs and become more densely populated. However, we continue to compete for survival and for the control of the arable areas that provide our sustenance. We instinctively continue to do so, for we are under the control of nature's influences and powers. By regulating our numbers according to the level of prosperity we wish to achieve, we can overcome the mastery of nature and the need to compete for survival. We are the most capable and must use our ingenuity and cooperate with each other to avoid the calamities that nature's competitive influences motivate.

We do not need intelligence to follow nature's course, but we have gained sufficient knowledge to realize the consequences of doing so. We know that we must live at peace with our own kind and in explaining how we can accomplish this, I hope to lead our industrious species from its present competitive course onto a trail where it can gain the means to earn to its hearts content. May we become ever more confident of our abilities as we hack our way through the jungle of fear and superstition in our endeavors to create the economic conditions that will bring peace and contentment to the human race.

Ancient man did not know where plants and animals came from, so was inclined to point at the sky in attempting to explain the unknown to his children. As a result, imaginative folk-tales evolved and have become our superstitious beliefs of heavenly powers. Those that incorporated sound survival values in conjunction with them thrived, and gained dominance over others; continuing to guide societies and set the course of civilization. When things went well it was claimed to be due to the helping hand of God, and when they went wrong the Devil was blamed. The spirits were claimed to be responsible for man's fortunes and misfortunes, and according to some enthusiasts, even determined how and when they would die. In accepting these ancient explanations as unquestionable our civilization blindly advances, not knowing or realizing the cause of its dilemmas, and failing to act in the necessary ways to prevent the final Armageddon.

Our religious teachings continue to overwhelm and dispute the conclusions that our modern scientific investigations support. These ancient and previously made explanations, set our minds at rest, and free us to attend to our daily tasks. As a result of our ignoring the scientifically obvious and factual explanations, our species has not been able to overcome the competitive influences that nature subjects it to. We have become more knowledgeable and wiser than the ancients, and are now able to conclude that earthly circumstances, rather than heavenly spirits motivate us to malign each other. It is the shortages that influence us to compete, and which drive us toward each other's throats. We must overcome these earthly shortages, so that we do not have to continue to compete over them. Conditions on earth have always been cruel to its species, for limited resources regulate their numbers. Our species can regulate its own numbers more humanely than nature does, and in avoiding the sorrows and wastes of war can prosper peacefully.

Modern day scientists have advanced our knowledge considerably, giving us a better understanding of environmental conditions. This has freed us from the unfounded presumptions and ancient superstitions that sought to explain the origin of the earth and the sanctity of our species. It appears that some of the heavier elements in our solar system are the result of more recent cosmic activity, suggesting that regeneration of new celestial bodies from the remnants of old is commonplace. It is not known how life actually began, but it has evolved into our present flora and fauna. Mankind is a part of this life and is related to other members of the animal kingdom. Our physical and cranial development is portrayed by our skeletal remains, and our technical advancement can be determined by our early tools and artifacts. The evidence of our development is not as complete as for other species that were more abundant or present for longer periods of time, but it is the only evidence that is available. There are gaps in our evolutionary chain as the result of the scarcity of remains, but we should not be confused because of it. Our modern day scholars describe the evolution of our species according to the evidence at hand, but the problem is that today's societies must discount this knowledge, for they have been unable to change their ways to conform to it!

As members of a competitive unit we cannot leave the group, and the group cannot reject its survival values which are embedded in its religious teachings. Our civilization's strong spiritual beliefs are not supported by the findings of our modern-day scientific investigations. However, they have remained inseparable from the survival values that they promote, and which our societies have required to maintain their competitive positions. When we find that we are distantly related to the primates, we must reject the fantastic and look for earthly and understandable solutions to overcome nature's hold on us. We come to realize that we have no soul that is distinctive from that of other species, and so have not been blessed with other lifespans. We come to realize that the popularity of beliefs which support reincarnation, or rebirth into a heaven where labor is not essential, is just plain wishful thinking. We come to realize that we have been blinded by the glow from the heavens, and cannot see what is at our feet. Our belief in a second life has been our only hope for the future, and we cannot visualize conditions more perfect, but we are on earth, and this is the only life we know anything about.

We have reason to believe that the powers of nature are uniform throughout the universe, exempting of course, the suspected presence of anti-matter and its surroundings. If there are other spheres on which life has established itself, that life would increase in numbers according to the nutrients that nature or natural conditions provided. Then those organisms would be forced to compete for survival, the same as they are forced to do on earth; and would be regulated by the environmental conditions on that planet, rather than by other imaginary influences.

On earth we found that promoting numbers provides additional strength to the nation, and we have survived and overcome others by following this practice. The right to life becomes ingrained in our philosophies, and the unable and the unproductive are prevented from perishing. Life is no longer exclusively dependent upon the productivity of an individual, and the incentives to produce have naturally become subverted. The true conditions on earth are such as nature and our environment provides, and we must continue to produce our needs for we have advanced beyond our hunting and food-gathering existence. We may willingly share our earnings with others, but the right to life is not supported by the powers of nature. Neither should it be promoted by a society that no longer needs the power of numbers to retain a numerical advantage. We must abandon the survival values that are no longer beneficial, and promote those that preserve our health and economic viability.

We are not the blighted creature that ancient superstition has portrayed, for we are the most intelligent and capable that nature has fashioned. The powers of nature cause all life on earth to compete for survival–we are no exception. We have now come to understand the hold that nature has upon us, and can avoid many of our competitive activities. In amalgamating our nations and providing ourselves with the opportunity to adequately fulfill our needs, we will be able to overcome nature's competitive influences and gain peaceful coexistence. It will take the expenditure of effort on our part, for we do not have a provider (except for nature), and we do not have a slave (except for the beasts we domesticate).

During the last few generations, with advances in transportation and communication; we gained the physical ability, but did not have sufficient knowledge to perfect conditions on earth. The League of Nations and the United Nations have failed us, for they have attempted to outlaw the aggressive acts of nations, rather than relieve the conditions that motivate them. International conflict is caused by pressures within a nation; so in order to have peace, the competitiveness which motivates the hostilities must be alleviated. That originates with the individual, and our leaders' acts usually correspond closely with their supporter's demands. Noncombativeness or noncompetitiveness must begin at the individual level, for our national contentions put our representatives at the peace table with little or nothing to offer.

If we did not try to exploit other nations, they would not have to protect their borders. Aggression, begins with the drive to gain fulfillment at the individual level, and is carried upward and shows its teeth at the political level. At that point, mankind's competitiveness is history, condemned by the masses, and misunderstood by those that were the cause of it all. However, in the past, societies have had no choice and no alternative to refrain from being competitive. They survived because of their competitiveness, and anything that reduced this competitiveness lessened their probability of survival and potential.

Rival nations have used, or are about to use, every weapon ever invented. Competition for survival is nature's way. The sensible approach is to teach mankind that it is possible as well as most correct to avoid our aggressions. If we can cause our societies to unite and respect each others economic independence, salvation will be ours!

We must teach societies to accept the knowledge that our civilization has discovered, for we are not living in dreamland. We must teach them the truth about our environment so they can deal with reality as it is, rather than as our theologians would have us believe. Then we can understand what our real problems are, and can deal with them effectively. We should hope that this science develops to the level of our other fields of knowledge. That the resulting change in course for enlightened man will not be into another blind alley but into a well-lighted street where it would be safe for those who are aware of the true nature of our problems, to lead us toward a paradise that would become more perfect as our knowledge and ability to perfect it increased.

What I recommend we do, can only be done by replacing our present competitive institutions with an administration that provides us with foreseeable advantages. We should deal with the source of the problem, which is economic, and which can be alleviated through the regulation of population and the safeguarding of our basic need to prosper unmolested. We are not trying to please the majority at the expense of the minority as in the political systems of today. We are trying to please everyone at the expense of no one, for the minority does not have enough to please the majority anyway.

With the upgrading of our economy, there would be sufficient opportunity for all who are concerned about earning their living. We would not be giving out free dinners, but those who are capable of profiting through exploiting our earthly resources would find the opportunity to earn their livelihood through honest toil. As individuals: we would keep what we needed from the past, and would support our charitable causes as they affected us. Additionally, we would discard that which we did not need or want, but we would not leave anything of worth behind. Consequently, we would carry the load of our choosing, and would not wish to be burdened with the refuse of others. Therefore, our new administration would not support from the public purse, what we as individuals refused to support from our own. We would also guard the public purse, for it is almost the same as our own.

The only assets we have are tangible. The rest are IOU's. It is this generation that has got behind and piled up the debt, and it is this generation that will get stuck with the paper. Our new world order will not be a continuation, but an alternative to our many opposing regimes. We will not pass the buck because there is no one to pass it to! Neither would we settle the debts between nations or with the world banking system. We would be starting with a clean slate, and we would start by not indebting anyone unjustly. However, individuals would not be starting anew. They would keep their tangible assets and continue to develop their technologies and provide themselves with the comforts and conveniences of their era.

When we unite the peoples of the earth, many will become unemployed through having worked in industries and occupations no longer needed. Others would lose their welfare and pension cheques, while still others would suffer from the devaluation of our monetary units. However, it is to be hoped that the transition into our new order would be at a speed that our societies could adjust themselves to. As we reduced our numbers, our per capita opportunities would increase so that we all should be able to earn enough for our needs.

It is we, who must cause and control the speed of change; and it is we, who must prevent an undesirable collapse of the economic system that provides our present means of subsistence. We do not wish our intellectual civilization to flounder, and for societies to have to begin again as they have had to in the past. We wish to preserve the technical advances that we have made, and to retain this knowledge and our assets, while we rebuild our social structure and governing system for a safe journey into the future. It would be much like building a new ship from the material of the old that is in danger of sinking. Our new vessel will not accommodate all of the cargo, but we cannot stop bailing until we have salvaged our assets and the valuable material that is above the waterline. The ballast or dead weight of our nonproducers, along with the bilge water which is the amount that we got behind in our bailing (and which is the debt that we left to the next generation to pay off) will be allowed to sink, leaving us with the material to build a new vessel that will float on its own and which we will be capable of steering in the direction we wish to go.

The only sensible course that we can chart is one which will fulfill our physical and mental requirements, and with responsible management we would definitely limit the number of passengers so that they would not have to fight over the space they needed. All of our offspring would have to be supported by their sponsors, and would eventually have to earn their keep and pay their share of the costs of operation. It is to provide adequately for our future comforts and well-being that we would do this, for it is those who put out the effort that are entitled to the benefits of their work. As a result of this realization there will be no free passes, or provisions for stowaways, or creeps in the closet.

We have everything we need on earth, but its arable area is limited. Therefore, we must take this into account when we attempt to improve conditions for our species. We do not need more exploitable territory, only the common sense and the desire to correct conditions so that we do not need to compete with others for the resources that we do have. With the amalgamation of nations: we will be freed from national controversies, and be able to control our numbers so that there is sufficient opportunity for all to fulfill their individual needs.

It is the gradual build-up of knowledge throughout the ages that has allowed us to become aware of the nature of our environment. Our place within it, with respect to nature, is of our choosing. We are the most capable species, and there is nothing to deter us from taking advantage of the opportunities that are before us. We should now be able to overcome nature's competitive influences, and in ending political discrimination and offering a level playing field, would dispel the usual objections toward uniting the societies of the earth. We have but one life to live and one planet to enjoy it upon. Reality forces us to accept these facts, and we can do naught but make the most of it. As we endeavour to ascend out of the pit in which nature confines its subjects, we must take the three vital steps that are necessary. First, we must unite our societies or nations and form a single authority. Second, we must formulate and abide by legislation that prevents discrimination and reduces competition at the economic level. Third, we must control our numbers so that we are not forced to compete for the quantity of earthly resources required to earn sufficient for our needs.

It is our unfounded spiritual beliefs that have prevented us from clearly understanding that it is the powers of nature rather than heavenly bogeymen that predestines all life on earth to compete for survival. These beliefs, in combination with values that enhance our competitive abilities must be laid to rest so that we can take the necessary steps to escape from nature's grip. The heights to which we can rise above nature's competitive compound will depend upon our ability to shed our rivalries. However, as the dominant and ruling species we will continue to exploit for our personal benefit, the other unfortunate critters that are not able to overcome the struggles and strife that natural conditions subject them to.

I cannot at present estimate how long it would take for our societies to take the necessary measures to avoid many of our competitive practices. My only objective is to clear the sky and shed some light upon the path that could lead us from the fate that nature has provided for us, to the peacefulness and plenty of a noncompetitive lifestyle. We, the most intelligent species on the face of the earth, will determine our objectives and therefore make the climb, for we have found the trail that leads to the betterment of our prospects on earth.[6]

With intelligent foresight and evasive action we should be able to overcome many of nature's competitive influences, and rise from the source of our damnation. There would no longer be a life and death race to advance our technology as there is in the present. Our curiosity for learning and the demand for new products would be the only incentive for our civilization to advance its technological abilities. Our challenges would remain before us, and we would continue onward toward improving our lot. We would still strive to further explore and exploit the universe, but our expenditures will probably be minimal. They would be financed by domestic industry, rather than by our present nation's efforts to stay ahead in the development of technology and in the arms race. Any frantic activity to explore the universe, has and would continue to be by those who had failed to find the solution to their problems on this planet. Maybe it is that which is in this book that they should be searching for.

The sun rises and sets, and the rains come down for the benefit of all that are present. We harvest nature's production and exploit its resources to supply our needs and wants. We have gained the ability and the uncontested right to administer the areas that fall within our grasp. No one tells us what or what not to do, for we are the almighty in the absence of a greater intelligence.

---

6. There are many ways that our species can be annihilated by natural cosmic events, but now we should be able to avoid helping nature do so.

10

A Quest for National and Political Unity

(Humanity's survival depends on it)

In the tranquility of a socially united world our survival would not be dependent on the might of numbers, or the increased use of military or environment-altering technologies. It would become dependent upon our physical ability to produce our needs in a honest manner, and our moral ability to refrain from confiscating and redistributing the profits of others. We will no longer need politicians to determine how best to appease the majorities at the expense of the minorities. We must become one, politically and nationally. One species attempting to better our circumstance through exploiting the planet's resources, while refraining from attempting to better ourselves through exploiting the productivity of others. We should no longer need or desire the middle-men, or political representatives that pay themselves generously for determining how best to appease their supporters to retain their parliamentary seats. They do not produce anything, and only tend to create controversies amongst us with their discriminatory legislation.

By eliminating the national and political divisions that cause riots and wars we could free ourselves from these previously unavoidable expenses, and gain the full benefits of our work. This would give us greater economic self-sufficiency and help overcome our need to prey upon the profits of others for survival.

We must regain the physical and mental ability to earn our livelihood through exploiting the resources of the planet. Our produce is the commodity that we generate in exchange for our work and it is not right for others to take or steal from us. Therefore, we should do our best to keep our personal earnings from the public's grasp. This we have not been able to do in our competitive environment; for the majorities have found it desirous to deprive the minorities of economic equality while they promote the nation's population densities, and its survival values.

In the presence of scarcities, we are forced to compete in order to survive. But in the presence of plentiful resources to exploit, we could more easily respect the earnings and assets of others. With no longer any need to support our present survival values to safeguard national interests, we could reduce our populations to the extent that there are plentiful resources for the use and prosperity of all.

With the discontinuance of governmental subsidies to politically favored groups, gays and lesbians would have the same rights as others. With no subsidization for the rearing of children or provision for spouses pensions, there would be no need for government to recognize or adjust its laws to accommodate sexual peculiarities. Medical technology that can create life outside of the womb and surrogate mothers, would have the same restrictions placed upon them. With each adult given one-half of a right to bring a new child into existence by whatever means they chose, our government could not be claimed to be pre-judicial.

Humanity and society have the power and the right to determine or adjust our survival values, so as to guide the course of civilization. The sperm, the embryo, and the unborn should not be given rights that contravene the necessity of regulating our numbers. Children and adults also should not be conferred rights that may hinder society's control of its destiny.

Humans have feelings and concerns for each other. They have the heart, the will power, and the ability to sooth their feelings. Government on the other hand, is an institution that does not have personal feelings. Therefore, it must remain neutral and refrain from condemning or promoting the inconsistencies of its citizens. Our society will on its own initiative find the economic methods that best support the continuance of life and the preservation of the environment--our administration is not smarter than those that form and support it. Our government must become the guardian for each and everyone. Our society, and hopefully an intelligent majority will continue to rule. They are the most powerful faction, and are free to push their weight around. Neither you nor I should be so foolish as to physically oppose the majorities wishes, but they must be confronted with the wisdom they are lacking so that they can correct their ways.

During the years that I raised cattle, I was their governor. I was not their god, for I could not protect them from the many perils that confronted them. As an unbiased governor, I would put my cattle on an acreage that had sufficient grass and water for their needs. In doing so, each animal was given the freedom to exploit the grasses to gain nutritional contentment. As their governor, their was no attempt on my part to discriminate amongst the beasts, so they had an equal opportunity to flourish. This is not to say that the cattle were equally endowed, or exploited the grasses in an equal manner, for some became more fat than others. Also their calves were not born equal, for some had mothers that produced more or richer milk, or were better able to protect their calves from marauding coyotes during the early months.

I see a comparison in how I looked after my livestock to how our new government should rule its subjects. Our government does not produce anything, and cannot provide us with an equal opportunity to exploit the resources of the planet. It can only enforce laws that limit our numbers, so that there is sufficient opportunity for all. It should not discriminate amongst us intentionally, or attempt to make us equally successful in our ventures, for some of us are smarter or are more ambitious than others. All we require is to overcome the shortage of earthly resources that cause us to compete for them. Allowing those with an able mind and body to prosper to the fullest. It is they that have the power to support the charitable causes of their choice, and to uphold survival values which prevent the over-exploitation and deterioration of our supportive ecology. It is they that must govern themselves to gain the peace and prosperity that is available to them.

In providing guidance to a species that is killing itself off, or should I say competing itself to extinction, the circumstances are opportune for those that wish to avoid their competitive fate. I assure you that there are no known influences present, other than the gentle persuasions of nature. We can bet our future on it.

11

Goodbye and Good Luck

(You have to make your own)

This is not the end—it is only the beginning. The beginning of a science that our generation and future generations will enlarge and perfect until it suits them, thereby fashioning our new moral and legal code which provides commandments that are advantageous and enforceable. These will bring us into an era where the motives for social violence are reduced and war is eliminated. God and the Devil will take their places alongside Santa Claus and the Tooth Fairy, and our erroneous philosophies would be superseded by one that does solve humanity's social and economic deficiencies. We will climb out of the pit where nature holds all of those that cannot escape its influences, and ascend above the dark clouds of superstition that have been blinding us, leaving our ethnic prejudices and our deplorable competitive existence behind. As we climb into the light of reality the trail that we must follow will become more clear, giving us the ability to gauge and circumvent the obstacles we meet. We can be assured that humans are now able to rescue themselves from their competitive progressions, and be thankful that we are not permanently destined to everlasting struggle and strife. We have but to use the knowledge that we have gained in order to better our prospects on this planet.

We may wish that humanity had begun to solve its economic disparities and competitive adversities much sooner. We then would not have damaged our ecology so severely, or depleted our natural resources to the extent that we have done. It has recently become more obvious that our civilization is nearing its end, not because of the inability of large segments of the human population to gain the required sustenance, for nature has always limited our numbers in this manner, but because of ecological disruptions as the result of contaminants and pollutants. It will take time to educate the masses so that they can overcome nature's competitive influences and guide the course of human civilization toward desirable objectives. Barring nuclear warfare, we will probably experience many institutional breakdowns and economic shortages that would decimate our numbers. We should come to understand the need to live in balance with the opportunities that our planet provides, and use our advancing technologies to produce the comforts and plenties we desire. Realizing that our life supporting ecology is very fragile, we will surely attempt to prevent its destruction. With intelligent foresight and evasive action, our species can become the beneficiary of its technology rather than the casualty of it.

12

An Afterthought or Two

(While humanity hesitates and contemplates)

It will take an informed majority to guide the course of civilization. It is the power of humanity, and not the power of spiritual omnipotents that can rescue us from our national and political contests to best each other. A wise and capable species must teach that which it can see and understand with its five senses, for that is the only reality that there is. The young and the old must be taught with all of the communication facilities that are available in order to counteract the various spiritual doctrines that are presently being promoted. In this way, the competitive injuries that the powers of nature cause us to commit upon each other can be avoided and our understanding of reality could guide us toward creating peace and prosperity for all upon this planet.

These essays are a first, in explaining how to overcome our competitive fate, which is caused by the universal forces we are subjected to. With this knowledge we should be able to live in balance with the territorial resources we require to gain con-

tentment and become able to act objectively in guiding our civilization in the direction we wish it to proceed in. This is a project that requires the participation of all. None must be allowed
to opt out and ruin the aspirations of the many. These theories
are no longer exclusively mine, they are now yours to consider
and promote. May they bring forth the understanding that is
required to lead humanity to the peace and plenty that they have
been praying for.

The earth and the universe should not be the resource that
a bunch of sapiens should continue to kill each other over, but
the resource that they should exploit to their best advantage. It
is all ours--there is no one that can take it from us. Use it and
be content, for it is all that we have.